Luminous Darkness

The Gateway to Understanding Opposites as Complements

Toni G. Boehm, Ph.D.

First Edition 2004

Luminous Darkness: The Gateway to Understanding Opposites as Complements

Inner Visioning Press
Greenwood, MO 64034
To contact the author: www.toniboehm.com or
816-537-5254 (F)
816-304-3044 (C)

Published by **Inner Visioning Press**
Printed in the United States of America

The publisher wishes to acknowledge the artwork of Leslie Bradshaw, the graphic design work of Gail Ishmael, and the editorial work of Mary Lou Kaltenbach, Jay Boehm, and Joni Wilson–without your help these words would still be locked in my computer.

ISBN 09701537-3-2
Library of Congress Card Number: 2003099330
Luminous Darkness/ Toni G. Boehm, Ph. D.

CONTENTS

ACKNOWLEDGMENTS

How does one begin to thank the Presence for the Graces It bestows? My heart is full of gratitude for the gifts that I have gleaned from my experiences with the feminine archetypes of universal consciousness and especially the archetype known as "the Black Madonna."

I am blessed by all, both men and women, who have an affinity for Her. It is obvious that we are drawn toward each other because of this resonance. On the other hand, there are also people in my life who do not understand this quest that I am on, to them I say: "Thank you too, for being my teachers; it is important to know when to stay quiet and you have taught me this."

To my husband, Jay—I love you!

To Priscilla Richards, how can I ever thank you for your friendship and all the treasures that you have shared me throughout the years. Librarian is your title, Mystic is who you are!

To Andrew Harvey, you are a jewel on my friendship hat.

To Rev. Ruth Mosley, a gentle and yet, oh-so-powerful woman, you can preach girl!

To Rev. Sallye Taylor, the first day we met, several decades ago, she told me that being cute wouldn't get me anywhere in the spiritual arena, I would have to learn to lead with my heart—I didn't have a clue what she meant!

To Joni Wilson, no words can express my appreciation for all the support you have given me.

To "The Girls of Summer"–Ann, Sandra, Carolyn, Kay, Fawn, Julie, and Toni C.–my daily swims with you were part of the alternative therapy that called forth the ultimate healing. Thank you for accepting me with such open hearts.

To my sister Rosalie and cousin Pam, I love you. Thank you for choosing me as your relative and more importantly as your friend.

To Jon and Rosalyn, Kim and Derby, Allison, Michelle and Robert, Amanda, Alexis, Lindsey, Lauren, Courtlyn, Joshua, and Connor–you are the legacy of our life shared here on earth.

To those women who have stood beside me through out the years: Susan Burnett-Hampson; Dawna Roberts; Marj Britt; Argentina Glasgow; Madaline Lawrence; Linda Spencer; Sharon Connors; Wendy Zender; b1 and b2 – a.k.a. Barbara Burnstein and Barbara Marx-Hubbard; Mary Omwake; Mary Tumpkin; Joan Borysenko; Dorothy Pierson; my aunt – Druscilla Quinn Smittle; the late but greats, my first Truth teachers Martha Guidici and Janey Paulson, my grandmother–Laura Jones Smittle, my mother–Eula Gene Smittle Fox, my aunt–Jeanne Smittle; my mother-in-law--Myrtle Boehm, and to all the other fabulous, juicy, sacred, special, and incredible women who have crossed my path and who have called themselves my friend, thank you for the wisdom that you have shared with me.

To all the friends who share my enthusiasm around the importance of reclaiming the feminine nature of the Divine, I love you. And to those of you around me who still don't have a clue as to what I am talking about—I love you, too!

Toni G. Boehm

PREFACE

"Wholeness...is not achieved
by cutting off a portion of one's being,
but by an integration of the contraries."
—Carl Jung

"I believe that the Holy Mother, the Divine Feminine,
is now being restored to her righteousness in the world
and that she will reign equal with Jehovah **[the Divine**
Masculine] *in the heavens and the Earth."*[1]
—Charles Fillmore: 1921, *Unity Tenet 16*

"Jesus reached the limit of his masculine consciousness ... he was
the light of the world, the heat of the world ... He could not
express Himself on that plane until He became the Holy Mother
... We have not that concept of the Mother."[2]
—Charles Fillmore, 1929 Sunday Lesson

"Darkness and Light dance: ... Darkness simply means 'what is
unknown' in Hebrew; light means 'what is known.' When we
allow ourselves to really listen to the 'other,' then darkness and
light dance and new creation is possible. When Darkness and
Breath [Light] make love, their child is Consciousness ... If
[we] simply allow [ourselves] to breath together, into [our]
shared ignorance of each other, then genuinely new solutions
could and would be born"
– Neil Douglas-Klotz: Abwoon 2004 Newsletter

Life is an ever progressive, upward movement of conscious evolution. As you meander through the landscape of the pages of this book you will be invited to share in the personal evolutionary journey of a soul on the path, making its way back Home. Through the medium of personal stories, experiences, initiations, meditations, exercises and revelation you will be provided with a primer for the mind and heart to begin to accept, deepen, and/or awaken already known information regarding the process of transformation and the role of the archetypal divine feminine in that process. The phrase that unfolded over time for me, which best describes the various nuances inherent within this described course of transformation, is Luminous Darkness.

Have you ever sat under the darkness of the night sky watching the luminous lights dance their way across the heavens? It was a moment such as this that brought to my awareness the idea of Luminous Darkness; Light inherent in Darkness. In a flash of blazing light that seemed to come from nowhere and everywhere, at the same time, I realized that opposites, in whatever form they appear, are not two polarities – each fighting for the right to be dominant – but opposites are in fact, one divine complement, each needing the other to complete their purpose. In a burst of discovery, I clearly understood–once we uncover the complementary nature of opposites – we are provided with the opportunity to unearth the essence of the gifts that each complement or so-called opposite comes to share with us. All opposites (Light/Darkness, Masculine/Feminine, Old/Young, Transcendent/Immanent, Good/Evil, and so on) exist in order that we might learn and/or be taught by them through seeing the contrasting nature of all things and then willingly holding those contrasts within the container of the mind, without judgment.

Through the act of looking at opposites, without judgment, we ultimately open the way to discover who we are at the core level of being, in our heart of hearts. Contrasts exist on this third dimensional plane of awareness as an aid to bring a greater sense of personal understanding and to awaken us to a deeper realization of the age-old question, "Who am I?"

Just as the answer to the question, "Who am I?" has multiple levels of meanings, definitions, and routes to discovery, so did I discern over time that this was true for the idea of Luminous Darkness. Once the concept of contrasts and complements awakened within me, a myriad of ideas about the deeper meaning of Luminous Darkness began to unfold, also.

As a dictionary's purpose is to define the multitude of ways that a word may be utilized in different contexts and situations; so too, is this book meant to do the same for the concept of Luminous Darkness. Thus, as you wander through the pages of this book, you will find that the words, Luminous Darkness, are used as a framework to define the following concepts, ideas and perceptions:

1. **Luminous Darkness**–the space where the creative substance of the universe hovers, awaiting the "call" to do Its work, to call forth creation.
    a. This idea is outlined in The Hebrew Testament, Genesis 1; "… and darkness was upon the face of the deep and the Spirit of God was moving over the face of the waters ... Then God said, 'Let there be Light.'"
2. **Luminous Darkness** – masculine and feminine energy. Historically and esoterically, Light and Darkness have been referred to as masculine and feminine-type energy. Light is considered masculine and Darkness is considered feminine.

a. Using a document entitled, ***"Unity Statements of Faith,"*** a series of lessons was given in the 1920s by metaphysician, E.V. Ingraham, and then repeated by L.E. Meyer in the mid-1940s. The ***Unity Statements of Faith*** document contained 30 foundational tenets, or statements of beliefs, which were penned in 1921, by pioneer metaphysicians, Charles and Myrtle Fillmore (co-founders of Unity School of Christianity, 1889). Lesson 1 discussed Tenet #16. The lesson shares insights on the secret of creation and the mystery of the masculine/feminine relationship in the creation process.

b. This lesson and Tenet #16, supports *Luminous Darkness* definitions 1, 2, 3, and 4.

c. Here is what E. V. Ingraham and then L. E. Myer shared about Tenet #16.

Tenet #16: (original wording from 1921)

"We believe that the Holy Mother (the Divine Feminine) is now being restored to her righteousness, and will reign equal with Jehovah [the Divine Masculine], in the heavens and the earth."

Tenet #16: (wording changed in 1930)

"We believe that Creative Mind, God, is Masculine and Feminine, and that these attributes of Being are Fundamental in both natural and spiritual man. – 'And God created man in his own image, in the image of God created He him; male and female created He them.'" (Genesis 1;26)

"Herein is the secret of creation. In this mystery of the male and female Principle is the process of all achievement. We begin immediately to think in terms of sex, man and woman. While men and women are an out-picturing of this Principle, Creation does not begin in the outer or visible. Principle is One, both masculine and feminine. Where the Principle is conceived in unity, Wisdom and Love are in perfect agreement; creation results.

In the Principle of Truth is involved the law of love or agreement which is the mystery of creation itself. The law of love or agreement is the law of life, the creative law of which everything comes into being. Science tells us how creation emanates from the activity of positive and negative electrons, male and female. Positive electrons move to the right, negative to the left. When these two meet there is friction unless there is agreement. Where there is agreement, there is a blending together, a new activity which results in a third force, or new creation.

When masculine and feminine forces meet, there is a bringing forth of a new force; they reproduce. The process is everywhere operative throughout nature...The male and female Principle, the force of Life that conceives Itself, and brings forth all creation. This Principle is the Christ in man, [it is] both masculine and feminine in nature, both Wisdom and Love..." [The lesson ended with Tenet #30]

Tenet #30: "Almighty Father-Mother, we thank thee for this vision of Omnipotence, Omniscience, and Omnipresence, in us and in all that we think, and do in the name of Jesus Christ. Amen."

3. **Luminous Darkness**–the "Silence." Luminous Darkness is the "inner shrine," the "womb-like space" within, which contains nothing and holds everything. Out of this space of emptiness, all is created and all is birthed.

   a. We take "pilgrimages to the shrine of inner darkness" each time we go within, in meditation, and wait for The One to reveal Itself through the darkness.

   b. One does not find this place of "Silence" in the outer realms of manifestation; it is touched only when one willingly sits at the inner shrine, in the midst of the mysterious, womb-like space of darkness. Of the all the definitions, some may consider Luminous Darkness, as the inner shrine of the Silence, the most important.

4. **Luminous Darkness**–the place, from which ideas originate; involving the realms of Superconscious and subconscious mind.

   a. When a Divine Idea is born within us, the Divine Substance of Light or Thought-Energy, stair-steps its way from the Super-conscious Mind (coming in its purity from 4th dimensional awareness or a higher frequency) through the matrix of consciousness, to the subconscious mind.

   b. In the subconscious mind, this Energy is shaped into thought forms–forms that are in harmony or agreement with the beliefs that we hold in the personal and collective consciousness of the subconscious mind.

   c. After this time of shaping, the idea is then projected into a denser form of materiality or manifestation, the conscious mind. At this point the person receiving the idea may experience a burst of inspiration–which is sometimes experienced as a flash of light.

   d. Divine Ideas (Light, Love, Peace, Harmony, Beauty, etc.) from the Mind of God (a.k.a., Source, Divine Energy, Light-Energy, the Birthing Place) can never be destroyed. However, they are diluted or diffused by the "stuck" or negative-type energetic thought-forms contained within our subconscious mind.

   e. These stuck thought forms or energetic blocks create–what psychological researcher Dr. Carl Jung refers to as–our "shadow or shadow-aspects of self." When these typically negative energetic blocks in the subconscious are cleared away, the Light is then free to shine through the sacred Darkness, as a star in the night sky, revealing the Glory of Its Essence into every facet of our life.

5. **Luminous Darkness**—the playground of archetypes, dreams, and symbols; involving the realm of the subconscious mind and the personal and collective consciousness.

a. Words are not the chosen language of the unconscious mind; its language is archetypes, dreams, symbols, and ideas. Most of us aware of the fundamental nature and energy of dreams, symbols and ideas, however, the healing energy of archetypes may be somewhat unfamiliar to us.

b. An archetype is a pattern of energy that is held in the collective unconscious mind and is recognized within our psyche for the pattern of energy, which it represents. These archetypal figures include the Wicked Stepmother, the Hero, the Princess, the Witch, the Martyr, the Divine Feminine, the Divine Mother, the Black Madonna and thousands more.

1. Most of the feminine archetypes referred to in this book are known as Black Madonna/s. These archetypal energies have had a profound effect on my life and in my healing process.

c. Archetypes, dreams, and symbols reside within the collective unconscious/subconscious mind of humankind and can be of tremendous assistance in our healing and transformative work. Carl Jung in his Collected Works impresses the importance of this process with these words:

"One does not become enlightened by imaging figures of light but by making the ... [the unconscious] conscious"

It has been said that the subconscious mind -- and the subject matter or thought objects "hidden" and contained within it -- is the best and most demanding teacher on the path to spiritual wholeness.

"Shadows are not created by Darkness; shadows are created by Light reflecting off "objects hidden" within the Darkness."

—T.G.B.

d. The subconscious/unconscious realm is the storehouse of events for both the individual and for humankind, a.k.a., race consciousness or collective consciousness.

e. The subconscious mind does not know right from wrong, it is only a repository of information. This information is "spit" back to us when we are confronted with the experiences of life.

f. Thus the subconscious mind can be the gateway for healing and transformation, when we are willing to embrace its contents by bringing the archetypes, symbols, dreams and ideas hidden within its depths, into conscious awareness.

g. It has been said that our true inner work begins when we are willing to call forth and confront the "shadow-aspects" of our self, the unconscious aspects of self, contained within the subconscious mind.

h. We say, "Yes," to participating in shadow work because we are ready to end our sense of suffering, to discontinue nurturing the illusions that we created about ourselves and to stop hiding from the truth of the magnificence of who we truly are as Energetic Beings and Energetic Information Systems.
i. Life, through its myriad of experiences, is designed to bring us to the realization that trying to be perfect is an illusion; for we can never meet perfection's costly expectation.
j. Perpetuating and living the "illusions" is very costly to our psyche and our soul.
k. "Conscious" evolution heralds the next phase of human development, thus, awakening to our Essence (the higher frequencies of consciousness) is the only viable alternative for the continued collective journey of humankind.

"The art of individualization, of becoming one's unique self . . . to discover who we are, we must ultimately withdraw those parts of ourselves which we have unwittingly projected onto others , thus learning to find deep within our own psyches the potentials and short comings which we had only seen in others."

--John Randolph Price: The Angels Within Us

During the years that I was doing research for, *"Luminous Darkness,* people often queried me as to why I would choose to use the word *Darkness* in the title. Their comments included statements like, "People don't like the word *Darkness*—it elicits a weird feeling." "People won't understand what you mean by *Darkness*." As I listened to these remarks, I began to think about what was really being said, underneath the words.

This is the conclusion I came to—the word *Darkness* conjures up thoughts based on an underlying sense of fear and evil. Fear of things that go bump in the night, of being alone, of being frightened, of being in sin, of causing sickness, unworthiness, poverty, and so much more—for all these conditions have been attributed to originating from some form of darkness or ignorance. Also, humankind fears darkness because we have been conditioned to equate darkness with a dread of some thing, some one, or situation. In addition, claims are often made that it is important that we shine the Light of goodness upon the darkness, leaving us with a feeling that Light is good and darkness is bad.

I would like to dispel these negative type thoughts associated with the word darkness and bring to light the idea that it is not darkness that causes the sense of fear or dread that is felt in these scenarios and situations, but ignorance. Ignorance is a state of a lack of understanding and of being unaware. In other words, we don't know what we don't know. Therefore, it would not be the darkness that we need to shine the light upon as much as it our own ignorance of that which we do not understand.

It is ignorance, the lack of conscious awareness around the truth of who we are as spiritual beings, that ultimately creates the human conditions we call, fear, sin, sickness, death, poverty, illness, want, attachment, and so forth—not darkness. We have mistakenly equated and mis-labeled ignorance as darkness. *Darkness* is the womb that holds the Mystery of an Idea, which *Light* will eventually birth.

Working with our unconscious/subconscious mind (*Note: the author chooses to use these words interchangeably throughout this work*) and the "shadow-stuff" (false beliefs and error thoughts that reside within the unconscious mind), reveals–NOT–our brokenness, but how we can become whole. Willingly embracing all aspects of our being, the negative and positive, through loving discovery and then lifting up these so-called negative or insecure aspects, we can call forth our power, competence, authenticity, success, beauty, intelligence, etc.

On my quest for inner knowledge, it has become clear to me that there this is only One Presence and One Power in this Universe. One Power, from which all 'derive their existence or reason for being.' The idea of two antagonistic powers in this Universe, being in competition with each other–e.g., Light vs. Darkness, God vs. Satan, or Good vs. Evil–is a basic mis-understanding or ignorance of the role of "God" (a.k.a., the Presence, Universal Energy, Higher Power, Source, or whatever your chosen word to describe this Energy may be).

Inherent in human nature is a need to control and understand everything, so as Adam did in Genesis we label things to prove that we are in charge of them, that we a have a sense of power over them, and that there might be an appearance or semblance of order. As long as we feel that things are in some type of an order, we feel that we have some type of control over them, albeit all this does is provide a false sense of security or feeling of authority.

Throughout the eons, humankind has labeled as "evil" things such as; individuals; races; cultures; storms with its raging fires, howling winds and explosive lightning; various animals; and a host of other "stuff." Yet all of these were just ideas that were misunderstood or different from the accepted belief of the day. Once it became clear to humankind as to what good these things could do for us (e.g. harnessing lightning for electricity) or, what they really were (e.g. darkness – the space of Mystery), we changed our opinion of them and gave them another label.

So it has been with the idea of darkness, we have labeled it, "not good." We have feared it, tried to run from it, and rebelled against it. Have you ever experienced sitting with a child that was afraid of the dark and did not want to go to sleep because it was dark? All their fears were wrapped up in the idea of what would happen to them if they were left alone in the midst of the darkness.

Fear of darkness lives in the collective psyche of humankind. Rather than embracing darkness, as the fertile soil of Creativity and all the gifts that it has to offer, we figure out ways to make it bad. And as a collective society, we have done that with everything that we did not understand.

Everything is energy, regardless of the form that it is in. Therefore when we label things (be it people, countries, objects, or emotions of fear, anxiety, anger, envy, jealousy, greed, hate, lust, worry and so on) as "not good or evil," we build up negative or destructive thought forces in our mind and end up attracting energy of a like nature to ourselves.

Once we understand the energy of opposites, we can begin to see the opposing forces for what they really are: complements to be worked with and not antagonists to be fought. This shift in perception, changes our life completely, for we begin to see through the eyes of wholeness and not separation. Wholeness knows the truth of our true nature, as children of Good. The sense of separation that we have come to feel comes from wandering in the shadows of the REAL and not the REAL Itself.

Time and time again, by bumping into and stumbling over the shadow-obstacles or shadow-illusions held in our subconscious mind, we have created a false sense around their reality and have given them power to influence our life. These self-created, so-called powers of bad, evil, jealousy, greed, control, anxiety, etc. will feel real as long as we continue to give them authority by believing in their reality to hurt us and feeling a need to fight them.

Let's look at the feeling of jealousy. Jealously only exists as a reality in life as long as we do not feel that we are worthy of love. Once we come into the realization that we are a channel of Divine Love, jealousy as a feeling or emotion disappears from our internal radar screen. The shadow-illusion, jealousy, is eradicated or released.

When we turn within and stand firm in the knowing that there is only One Power at work in our life and that Power will call forth the Good inherent in all situations, we will see a shift in our experiences begin to take place. The shift does not take place because we are denying the existence of some "thing" in our life, because "stuff" does happen; to do that would be very Pollyannaish thinking. The shift in our experiences takes place because now we see that these things that we thought were a power are not and thus, have no "real" power to hurt or hinder us personally or our lives in general. Everything, person, or experience in our life has only the power and life that we assign to it, through our thoughts and perceptions. When we change our thoughts/perceptions, we change our world.

It is the premise of this book that when we begin to consciously embrace and work with the various concepts that *Luminous Darkness* underpins, we commence upon a journey that leads to the unveiling of untold "secrets" locked within. When we willingly participate in the "work" that unlocks the shadows hidden in the subconscious mind, we open the way for higher frequencies of energy to move through us and to carry us upward (or downward, depending upon your view) on the evolutionary spiral of consciousness.

In addition, I personally believe, that there comes a time on the journey when we must consciously begin to embrace the feminine nature of the Divine and the various archetypes that that embracing calls forth. My personal journey was assisted tremendously by the feminine archetype of the Black Madonna. Through conscious participation with these energies, I was awakened to aspects of my being, which ultimately changed my life forever!

In the name of the One,

Toni G. Boehm, (T.G.B.)

INTRODUCTION

Luminous Darkness: The Gateway to All Understanding

"And I said to the [wise-woman] who stood at the gate of the [new] year:
'Give me a light that I may tread safely to the unknown!'
And [She] replied:
'Go to the darkness and put your hand to the Hand of [the One].
That shall be to you better than light and safer than a known way.'
So, I went forth, and finding [Her] Hand,
Trod gladly to the [New Year and the Mystery of the Unknown.]"
—Minnie Louise Haskins: *The Gate of the Year [adapted]*

"True consciousness has two wings...
A bird with just one wing will fall flat on its face;
Even if it fights to get up, it'll only fly a few yards."
—Rumi: *Mathnawi* — *Teachings of Rumi* by Andrew Harvey

Birth Through Death: Awakening to the Mystery of Luminous Darkness

In November 1990, I was called unexpectedly to my mother's bedside. She had become very ill and within a few short days, she made her transition. As I sat with her during those last few hours, I reflected on the turbulent relationship that we experienced as we walked through this lifetime together.

In my earlier years, I had held biased and judgmental attitudes toward her, all built around my resentment of what I believed she had "done to me." I adhered to the belief that she had no other "real" purpose in life, except to make me miserable. After all, she was not educated, she did not work, she couldn't take care of herself or family, and she was mentally ill (her illness surfaced when she was 28 years old and I was 10). Also, from that skewed childish perspective, it seemed that she was home and gone and home and gone (back to the mental institutions) as often as the moon waxed and waned. And as a by-product of that movement, my life was being destroyed.

As I held her hand, memories from the past years flooded my being. As I reflected on those times, I realized how many precious years I had wasted disliking her so intensely. Now here we were with our time together coming to an end. As I looked at that frail, little body, a few tiny remnants of deeply buried unresolved feelings came up for my review. As they surfaced, I observed each one and chose to bid them ado. They melted away like ice in the hot sun.

She looked so small and helpless; I wondered how I could have expended so much energy trying to run from her. As she lay there, still and unresponsive, I felt the need to pour out my heart to her. I shared with her words and stories that I wished I had shared before. Regrets filled my being as I read my favorite poetry and sacred writings to her unconscious shell. I hoped in some way that the message would penetrate her comatose state and that she might know, even better, this person that she had given birth to. My heart filled to overflowing with love, as I looked at this woman who had chosen to be my mother.

Throughout the last few years of her life, we had made progress in healing our relationship, or I should say—I had made progress, for I now know that I held all the issues—but in this moment, that all seemed like drivel. An awareness of truth flooded my being. Although I had made my peace with her and considered her one of my best friends, I still had not in any real way ever tried to reach out to get to know her, to understand her dreams, her hopes, and her desires or to know who she was as a person and as a woman. How sad, my heart lamented, that we were brought together to share a lifetime together and we did not have the opportunity to touch at that deepest level of intimacy—Love.

With that realization and from that moment on, my spiritual path took a turn that led me to new territories and unimaginable depths of exploration of the mystery, magic, and mysticism of the Universal Presence. The incidences surrounding my mother's transition created a space for a spiritual initiation. This initiation awakened within me an awareness of the "veiled" side of the spiritual journey.

This book shares a detailed description of my experiences on the journey of "renting the veils" of illusion and appearance; with this process being assisted by the energies of the archetypal feminine. Any shards of wisdom that might be found within the pages of this book are derived from the sagacity that naturally emanates from the events and experiences that evolve out of traversing the spiritual path.

The spiritual transformations I experienced have led to new insights about the nature of spirituality and innovative ways to apply its teachings to everyday life. However, of all that I have gleaned and received from the years that I have consciously walked the spiritual path, undoubtedly for me the greatest gift that I can say that I have received is the discovery of my "other wing;" the conscious *realization* of the archetypal qualities of the feminine nature of the Divine, and their role in the evolutionary process of humankind.

I found that this "living" archetypal energy resides veiled and protected in the deep recesses of our subconscious mind and when once revealed, it comes forth in a multitude of forms and personifications. It has been through my conscious awakening to Her presence, as an aspect of myself that I have been able to go within and do the deeper work of clearing "shadow stuff". Without Her influence and inspiration, I might well have never discovered how "the shadows" were running my life.

Of all the "feminine face[s] of God" that I met along the journey, the ones that had the most impact on me and affected my life most significantly were those feminine archetypes* known as The Black Madonna.

****An archetype is a pattern of energy that is held in the collective unconscious mind and is recognized within our psyche for the pattern of energy it represents. Other archetypes that might be familiar to you are those of the wicked stepmother, the hero, the martyr, the princess,***

The Black Madonna, as an archetype, connotes an energy that carries the power to transform and heal, whereas the wicked stepmother as an archetypal energy implies a warning to be wary.

Silently from the interior depths of my being, this Black Madonna made Herself known to me (appearing in a multitude of forms and versions), She challenged me to shift from linear thinking to a more inclusive and intuitive way of looking at life. Her energy opened me to new vistas of awareness, granted me the opportunity to reclaim the hidden, shadow aspects of my being and most importantly, allowed my spirit to take flight.

The archetypal family of the feminine holds the energy of life, death and rebirth. Which can be translated to change, healing, and transformation; She can be called on for help in any of these areas, at any time. When the archetypal feminine, e.g., Black Madonna enters one's life, whether it is through a dream or an introduction of another kind, She begins to make Her presence known through the process of transformation, for something in our life begins to change or shift. Suddenly, we find that we are in the midst of an unexpected new beginning or an ending of something familiar—we are in the midst of a birth, a death, or a rebirth experience.

Our work during these times of change is to learn to trust that our experiences are our "teachers" and that also the teacher may appear physically or non-physically, depending on what is necessary for us to learn in order to take us to the next level of awareness. However, it is important to remember that it is always our choice as to whether we accept or reject the lesson inherent in the experience.

Back to the last moments with my mother...as I sat in that hospital room looking at her face, I began to review the many junctures of my life. I realized that each step I had taken was a direct result of the imprinting that I had received as I was growing up, from both my mother and my family—and that it was all good—regardless of the appearances.

I thought about my birth and how much my parents had wanted a boy. My grandfather on my dad's side was going to give them $500 if their baby was a boy. Well, I wasn't, so they didn't get any money and this was during a time when money was very tight. I thought to myself that my parents must have felt a great disappointment around this incident, and I wondered if I had unconsciously picked up any of that disappointment in one form or another along the way.

As I thought about this, I realized that I had always tried to please and appease my parents; I (unconsciously) never wanted my parents to be disappointed in anything I did. So I did the next best thing to please them, I brought out the masculine nature of my personality, submerged the feminine, and worked hard to be successful in everything that I endeavored.

The corporate facet of my life gave me the opportunity to develop, even more, the masculine side of my personality, and with it to adopt the attitudes that go with the dominator model of life. I loved the aggressive behavior of powerful men when I was in their midst. I abhorred sweet little sniveling women who acted like they couldn't do anything by themselves. My persona was that I was in charge. I knew what I wanted and I went after it. I enjoyed the hunt, the chase, and the kill. What I didn't realize at the time was that I was sacrificing my feminine qualities to carry out these traditionally male roles of power, aggression, and success. I allowed the pendulum to swing too far in the other direction and lost sight of the fact that what we need is neither all masculine nor all feminine, but a vital balance of the two.

This quest for balance revealed itself in my life through several channels. The first and most significant one was my relationship with a man I met in church. He was a deeply spiritual person, extremely kind, gentle, loving, and he also happened to be a corporate executive. When we met I had not yet begun my journey to the feminine nature of the Divine and had not explored at any depths a relationship with the Black Madonna. He was a teacher for me, for he was not afraid to nurture or to express his feminine nature. In a real sense he was my introduction to the feminine aspect of the Divine. After a three-year friendship, we married.

Another revelation came in 1987 in the form of a job change. I had earned a master's degree in nursing (1981) and was doing quite well in the corporate world, but I knew on a soul level that it was time for a change. As this was stirring in my heart, I discovered that Unity School of Religious Studies, at Unity world headquarters, was engaged in a search for a dean of administration. The skills required were precisely those I had developed in the corporate world. Three months after being hired, I was enrolled in the ministerial school. Although I had been on spiritual paths for several years already, ministerial school began to open me to a greater sense of understanding what the inner transformation is all about and I began my own.

In the midst of this gradual inner transformation, I began to receive phone calls that, ultimately, would speed my transformation immeasurably. The calls were from my mother. "Honey, I am not feeling well," she would purr to the phone, "but it is not anything for you to worry about." My mother had always been "sickly" so I tried to buoy up her spirits as I prayed with her. Being in and out of a hospital was not anything new for her. It was two weeks before Thanksgiving when she called the last time. We had our usual conversation. She was in the hospital again, but our conversation ended with her assuring me not to do anything because we would be together in less than two weeks.

I had just hung up the phone and rested my head back on the chair with a sigh of resignation when I heard the Voice. It came from the depths of my being. It said, "Go now!" The words were spoken in such a soft, compassionate, feminine tone but with such a force of authority behind them that they shook me to my core. I took a few minutes to pray, and then I ran to the bedroom to share with my husband what had happened. I knew that I had to leave that day. He didn't quite understand, since we had already made arrangements to leave a week later, but he readily agreed to leave with me later that afternoon.

When I arrived at the hospital, several hours later, I was shocked at what I saw. Mom was very ill, and with my master's degree in nursing, it didn't take me long to assess her deteriorating condition. For the first time I realized that my dad and my youngest sister were in a state of total denial about the gravity of her condition.

I spent hours with my mother over the next few days. It was the most excruciating experience that I had ever had in my twenty years of nursing. Mother had smoked for nearly fifty years—two packs of Lucky Strikes a day. Although she was only sixty-three, she was at the end of her time; the cigarettes had taken their toll. She held my hand, the oxygen going full tilt, and begged me to help her breathe. From a sense of deep agony and pain she whispered to me, "Help me, darling, I can't breath. Please do something for me."

I felt absolutely helpless watching my loved one leave this plane and knowing that in no way could I help her with her last request. She was so little, so defenseless and disabled, that my heart was being torn just watching her. Could this small bundle of skin and bones begging me for help be the same woman I had spent so many years hating? I was overcome with shame for not seeing the beauty of her being earlier.

We shared our deepest feelings as she lay on that hospital bed, as she took what would be her last breaths of life in this form. A day later she went to a coma and I was relieved. She was finally at peace. The doctor came in and told the family that we had to make a decision about whether we would put her on life support. If we did, she could stay in this state for years. My step dad, my two sisters, myself, and a few other family members wrestled with the decision. My step dad said it was up to me. As a nurse and now an ordained minister, I was the expert.

My siblings wanted to abdicate all responsibility for the decision, so the burden fell on me. The weight was absolutely unbearable. How do you pull the plug on someone you spent years hating without feeling traitorous guilt? Nothing comforted me. I prayed and pleaded with God to give me a sign, to speak to me, but no Voice came this time. We had heard the facts and I had to say something. In that final moment, I felt the words inside my heart: "Let her go." That's what I decided to do, and no one disagreed.

Letting go didn't happen over night, however. It took days, during which we sat waiting for Mom to release her soul to a higher plane. After nine agonizing days, our vigil ended and Mom slipped quietly away.

After her transition, we tried for two days to find a minister to do her memorial service, but it was Thanksgiving and everyone was tied up. I told my husband and step dad that if no one else would do her memorial service, then I would do it myself, and I did, creating her entire service around a simple poem called "Celebrating Life." At the beginning of the service I was surprised at how many people showed up to pay their respects to a woman who hardly ever left her house, and who I thought had no friends. But they all said the same thing: "Oh, how your mother ministered to me. She would call me at the right moment, when I was sad or feeling low and she would sing to me. 'You Are My Sunshine' was her favorite song."

As I began the service, the open casket to my right, I stood and spoke: "We are here to celebrate the life of Eula." All of a sudden I began to choke in mid-sentence, as if the words were stuck in my throat. At the same moment, a wave of weakness flooded me and I felt that I was going to collapse. It was as if someone had pulled the energetic plug within me. I had spoken her name, but I knew nothing else was going to come out. I cried out from within, "Help me, God. I cannot do this."

What happened next felt as if time stood still and I was standing back watching it all. As I stood there reeling, I saw a Light jump out from my mother's casket. It went to my youngest sister and then came over to me. It came up through my being and bathed me in the most glorious shower of light that I had ever felt. The light surged through me and went out through the top of my head. As the energy exploded through the crown of my head, I heard these words in my mother's voice, speaking to me through the interior of my heart:

"In my life I gave you birth. In my death, I give you rebirth."

I knew in that moment that the Holy Spirit, the Holy Mother, was baptizing me to a new level of living and being. Just as Jesus was baptized in the Jordan by the Holy Spirit, which heralded the initiation of his ministry, so too was I being prepared for mine—only I didn't know it! Little did I know that from this moment on, my spiritual life would explode and my spiritual journey would take an irrevocable turn. The sacred path that I had been traversing for nearly 15 years (at that time) now had a new Way Show-er and Guide; it was the Divine Mother.

The service went on and we ended by singing to one another just as my mom would have wanted it: "You Are My Sunshine."

A Madonna Moment

Throughout this book you will find headings designated: ***A Madonna Moment***. These are poems, stories, reflections, contemplative thoughts, and ruminations which are meant to pull the readers inward to elicit insights (and questions) on their lives and experiences. As you come upon the — ***A Madonna Moment*** — consciously relax, take a deep breath, and allow the words to feed your heart and soul with new thoughts and insights.

Embracing and Listening

In the midst of the mire of life's experiences,
The "Still Small Voice" speaks to me.
"Are you ready to begin to fully embrace the gifts that the
Experiences of your life have come to share?"
I take a breath and ponder the depths of this question.
Suddenly I feel something stir within me and
I realize that I am willing to live my life differently.
Facing my fears rather than running from them,
I see how in the frantic running to and fro,
I have forgotten who "I Am."
Stopping and taking time to embrace life and to listen to its rhythms
I live from a state of Grace and "In-lightenment."
— T. G. B.

Crossing the Threshold into Unknown Terrain: The Black Madonna Appears as a Guide

My first introduction to the feminine archetypes came in the form of a dream. The dreams' focal point was a dark-skinned woman, albeit, I did not know what She represented. The dream occurred in January 1990, several months prior to my Mother's transition. In the dream an unknown dark-skinned woman is suddenly standing in my living room; She extends her hand, which I accept, then escorts me to the basement of my house.

We journeyed down the stairwell in darkness, but I was not afraid. Much to my surprise, when we arrived in the basement there was an incredible amount of activity going on. The dark-skinned woman took me to meet several other dark-skinned women, each one unique and beautiful in her own way. We reached the place of the Wise Woman, the head of the group. She was old and not very elegant; however, her beauty shone from deep within.

She offered me the opportunity to make a phenomenal amount of money if I would allow them to continue working in my basement, making their product called "Miracle-Grow." I looked around and decided to say yes to their request. The yes was not based on the offer of money, but on the trust that I felt about the type of work these women were performing. The journey to the depths of who I was had begun, albeit I was not fully aware that that was what was going on.

Shortly after this dream, I began studying the history of the Goddess culture. These studies revealed that there was a time, starting as early as 50,000 years ago, when "God wore a feminine face." During this period, the deity of the people whose image was revered, honored and exalted, was feminine. In these cultures, which archaeologists now suggest flourished in Southern Europe, Mesopotamia, and parts of North Africa, the Mother Goddess was universally worshiped as the source of all life, and women, through whom all human life flowed into existence, were held in high regard. Yet, for almost 6,000 years now, that Mother-Goddess image has been pushed aside and replaced by a mindset that worships a transcendent male God, only.

By the time 1990 rolled around, there were only a few spiritual teachers discussing the possibility of the re-emergence of the Divine Feminine – there were lots of feminists, but very few were making the leap and connecting the dots back to bridging the feminine and masculine nature of God and thus, self. In fact, a paganistic, earth-based spirituality study and worship, was in the forefront; and God, in a masculine form, was often taboo to mention.

Being fortunate enough to awaken to the essence of both messages, I began to teach and facilitate women's retreats with the idea of merging the concepts of, "Awakening the Divine Feminine Within" and "Awakening the Secrets of the Ancient Goddess." I was clear in my teachings that desiring to study the Goddess and the Divine Feminine was not about taking a stand that says, "I hate men," nor were the gatherings or retreats to be feared as a group gone wild. I was making a statement about an inner longing that lives on in our cellular memories. A long-suppressed memory of times past that is alive in the collective unconsciousness. Through these experiences I found my "other wing" and I felt free to fly.

Throughout my life I had been fighting an internal war, trying to suppress the feminine side of my being because I believed it to be less than my masculine state. Now I was being given permission to embrace both. I could stand as a woman with highly developed masculine tendencies and aspects and still honor my feminine nature and the great gifts that it bestows to those whom are ready to receive. I realized that I did not have to sacrifice one to have the other. It was not an either/or it was a both/and.

As usual, once you have a deep realization or knowing, an experience comes forth to help you anchor the gift of the lesson—into consciousness. My experience came in this form:

A friend stopped by my office at Unity Village and shared with me an astonishing account of something that had happened to her while she was visiting Walter Starcke's Guadalupe Ranch on the Guadalupe River in Boerne, Texas. Shortly after she arrived, Walter invited her to visit the grotto located on his ranch. The grotto, dedicated to the Black Madonna in the form of Our Lady of Guadalupe, is a cave-like structure built to the hillside. As my friend entered the grotto and while her eyes were adjusting to the darkness, she caught her first glimpse of the Madonna.

Immersed in the darkness, inside the depths of this cave-like earthen structure, she heard the Black Madonna begin to speak to her. She felt the energy of the Madonna pierce her heart with love and her eyes filled with tears. With each tear that came, she felt as if years of "unknowing" were being washed away. Something shifted within the depths of my friend's heart-space and she knew it!

I listened intently to my friend as she shared the story of her adventure with the Black Madonna; what she was saying resonated in me. I was mesmerized by her words. Suddenly, I felt energy began to stir within my soul, and as if a sharp object penetrated heart I felt a burst of Light arise from my heart area. From that moment on I, too, was changed.

I haunted the Unity library and bookstore, and devoured all the books and articles I could find on this "new feminine archetype," that was previously unknown to me. Immediately, pictures of the Black Madonna in Her various forms started to come to my awareness and into my possession.

Kali, the Hindu Goddess of transformation, change, and destruction, was the first Black Madonna to make an impression on me. I was afraid of Kali, yet I felt compelled to know her mysteries. I wanted her to share her secrets and treasures with me, even if meant "danger." After all, she is known as the destroyer. What she destroys, however, is our vices.

My quest to know the Black Madonna led me to take pilgrimages throughout the United States and Europe and to attend retreats and sacred ceremonies. Once I attended a retreat in a cave because I desired to sit in the womb of darkness of the

Great Mother, Earth. The inner strength and power I found there in the darkness of that womb-like structure gave me the courage to participate in a fire walk, during which I defied the elements of nature. I traversed the hot coals without a burn and, more importantly, without being afraid. I realized afterward that the experience of defying the elements was an outer symbol of an inner ability to walk through and overcome the fears that I held in my mind—both consciously and unconsciously.

In initially accepting the idea of living within the spaciousness of paradox—of not having to choose sides—I have learned to fearlessly accept the foibles of the human condition. To know that everything does and will change and to take everything that life brings to me and to use it for the highest good.

Over the years, the feminine nature of the Divine (as the Divine Mother, the Black Madonna, The One with a Thousand Names) has beckoned me to come to Her, to learn more of Her mystery and to enter Her darkness without fear. What you will find in this book is a variety of ways, through the use of meditations and exercises, to begin the journey of entering the realm of luminous darkness without fear, for remember – you are never alone on the journey!

A Madonna Moment

Along Came a Spider

It was a warm summer night; the full moon was shining on the meadow, creating a luminous glow. Through the black of darkness, the trees blushed with an iridescent sheen and the flowers surrounding them appeared to stand at perfect attention. If we listened closely, it was almost as if we could hear nature singing and sharing the thought, "We honor that which is about to take place here on this sacred ground."

Fifty-six women came together that night, years ago, outdoors in what felt like a Secret Garden. We came together, drawn in the name of the feminine nature of the Divine and in the name of honoring of our own innate *Wisdom*. Gathered in a circle, each quietly prepared for the ceremony that was about to take place. This ceremony, an ancient rite more than thousands of years old, has been called by many names—a Croning Ceremony, a *Wisdom* Ceremony—but I choose to refer to it as a Wise Woman Initiation Ceremony.

Participation in this ceremony was strictly voluntary; any woman who was ready to proclaim the truth of their inner wisdom could join in. I have always felt that when one participates in this ceremony it is signaling to the soul—whose language is that of symbols and archetypes—"I am ready to announce the arrival of my *Wisdom* years, and I am willing to move into them with conscious awareness."

Thus, this ancient ritual is an outer symbol that indicates an inner readiness for change. As if to acknowledge agreement, the creatures of the night were singing loudly their nocturnal tune and the rhythm of their various songs felt as if they were chanting in harmony with us. Sounding an affirmation with that which was about to occur.

I was the facilitator of this gathering, and it was the first time that I had been called to perform this ceremony outside of my own local area. (However, as of this writing I have now initiated over 1,800 women into their *Wisdom* years.) As preparation for this special event, I spent the afternoon in prayer and meditation; desiring only that I would be used as a vessel, an instrument to the Glory of the Great Spirit, the One.

Thinking that somehow I might use them in the weekend retreat, I brought with me a deck of cards. Not just any cards, mind you, these were special, for each one had drawn on them, a power animal. I had always been taught that a person will innately know when they are ready to receive the gifts that their power animal represents. It is that knowing, that signals when the Power Animal card should be selected. The following is my experience of how I received my power animal:

Interestingly, I had had my Power Animal cards for years, and as much as I had used them in ceremony – I had never been drawn to select my own power animal. On the afternoon, of night that we were going to the Secret Garden, I received guidance that it was time to select my power animal. I prepared a sacred space for the cards and gently, arranged them on the table, face down. With my hands, palms down, over the cards, I closed my eyes and prayed. I asked the Great Mother Spirit to draw to me my right and perfect power animal. Slowly, I allowed the energy in the room and in the moment, to move my hands around the deck. Hovering over a place that pulled my hands to a stop, I dipped down and drew a card from the deck.

Still with my eyes closed, I gently held the card for a few moments between my hands. I sat with my power animal enclosed in a circle of love between the palms of my hands, next to my heart. I invited my power animal to be with me and asked that she teach me what I needed to learn for her powers. I then opened my eyes and looked at my card.

The card I drew was the spider. Big as day, there she was, sitting in the center of her web. "A spider," I moaned. "I don't want a spider as my power animal. I hate spiders!" "Surely there must be a mistake," I thought. I wanted to draw again, but something wouldn't let me. Inside I kept hearing the "Voice" say, "Listen deeper. I know what you are ready for."

Taking the book that accompanies the Power Animal cards, I decided to read what it had to say about this symbol. Here is a paraphrase of what it said:

"The spider is one unto her own, she is totally self-contained. She needs no outer source to acknowledge her power or authority. She creates her world from within her own being and then sits in the center of her creation, awaiting her good."

"Oh, well," I thought, "let me surrender to this. Maybe the spider has what I need, or at least what I am ready to claim." I closed my eyes and began to ponder the deeper meaning of this message. With each breath, I felt myself going further to the center of my being, the center from which all things emanate – just like the spider. Slowly, a flush of warmth caressed my body and I realized that there was a message for me, in this spider animal.

It was both a very personal message and I dare say, it felt as if it was a message for women in general. "I saw" how we (especially women over the age of thirty-five) from childhood were (and in many ways still are) bombarded with messages from society and family that shaped an orientation that taught us to look outside ourselves for acknowledgement, authenticity, and for someone with a greater authority.

I thought how innocuous it seems to teach children to look outside themselves for authority, particularly when this way of being is woven directly to the fabric of our psyche, as a societal norm. Add to this that the inherent tendency of women is to be relational; they desire to be in relation, with those around them and will often subjugate who they are, to be in relationship.

I knew that it was true that there a great tendency, for women, to give their power away to those that they are in relationship with, especially when in the collective unconscious of humankind there is an unspoken expectation of the male–female relationship. For in the collective unconscious mind, which reflects itself in society as a whole, lives the idea of male dominance. The male-dominant concept goes back thousands of years and is underpinned by religious tradition.

Yes, indeed, I myself had fallen into this trap. Especially with the men around me. I was always looking to my husband, my dad, my teachers, my minister, my boss, or anyone who I perceived was a "higher authority," for the answers to my questions of life. Answers, which I realize now, I had within myself all along.

Yes, Mother Spider, had come to teach me something, to give me a gift—it was the gift of understanding that all I need is within, that I create my world from within myself. I am my own authority; I need no other outside authority.

I did not at that moment have a clue as to the depths of what this realization would mean later in my life. For now, all I understood was that I *had to learn* how to be totally self-contained, totally sufficient in Self.

What this meant to me was that ***all*** the qualities of masculine and feminine of the Divine, were primal elements inherent within one's being and they were "alive" and "living" within me. These elements or qualities are the ***Splendor***, which Robert Browning refers to the "imprisoned splendor."

"***Truth lies within ourselves: it takes no rise from outward things...to know rather consists in opening out a way whence the imprisoned splendor may escape than in effecting entry for light supposed to be without.***"

My work now was clear, to learn how to release these qualities; no longer could I look to someone else to provide them for me. I knew that if I had looked to my husband for strength, now I had to learn to be that strength. This would require spiritual discipline.

I would have to practice self-honesty in every moment; I would need to be consciously aware of my expectations for my relationships to really look at what it was that I wanted them to provide for me. For whatever I had looked for in another, now I had to allow it to take expression from within me. All of it, whether it was protection, strength, wisdom, courage, understanding, love, a source of supply, my perceived good—regardless of what it was—was within me, and I could access it to create my world.

The ceremony was beautiful; it was as if the Great Mother Spirit shined Her countenance upon us, for everything was perfect. Each woman took her turn walking through a trellis that sat in the middle of the herb garden in the center of the meadow that was nestled between great evergreen trees. It was a walk of conscious intention; indicating for each woman, a willingness to accept her innate *Wisdom* and the ensuing change that this special *Wisdom* brings with it.

I waited on the other side welcoming each one in to her new awareness, her way of being in her world, and more importantly, her way of being with herself. As the women passed through the trellis, each one would stop in front of me; we would look into each other's eyes and I would anoint her forehead with special oil I had brought back from an ancient feminine site in Europe. After the anointing, the woman would join her friends and companions standing on my left, recreating a new circle on this side of the trellis.

Although we started the evening with this chant, without direction the first woman through the trellis began to softly sing, again, the melodic strains of, "*Ancient Mother.*" As each woman came through, they too then added their voice to this sacred chorale.

When the last woman came through, I had just finished anointing her forehead with oil, when she looked up and told me not to move. She called for the other women to come over and see what had happened. There between the top of my head and the trellis, a spider had woven a web and She was sitting right smack dab in the middle of it.

I stood unable to speak for I was in a state of pure awe and wonder. I only had one thought—"God is so good. Yes, She is!"

Feminine Archetypes "Live" in the Collective Unconscious

"Our ancient, battered, much-loved, little understood
Black Virgins
are a still-living archetypal image
that lies at the heart of our civilization and has
a message for us."
—Ean Begg: The Cult of the Black Virgins

"The unconscious also includes the dea
abscondita, the Black Madonna,
the goddess who has chosen to hide herself
in order to protect humanity from the
devastating consequences of killing her."
—Marion Woodman: Addiction to Perfection:
The Still Unravished Bride

"Perhaps the most powerful and all-embracing of all symbols...'returning' to our...consciousness to help us re-imagine the power of the Divine feminine is that of the Black Madonna....Seen in its full splendor, the image of the Black Madonna is one of the most moving and profound images of the Divine Mother ever imagined by humankind...And because the fullness of the Divine feminine is represented in the image, when we contemplate it fearlessly we are gradually initiated through it to the full nature of our Christhood in her"[4]
–Andrew Harvey: Son of Man:
The Mystical Path to Christ

For many people, the journey to the unknown arena of the subconscious mind has been led by the archetype of the Divine Feminine, who reveals Herself as a Black Madonna—also known by the ancient title of—"The One Goddess with a Thousand Names."

Marion Woodman, in *Dancing in the Flames*, states that ***"For men, the dark eternal woman in her many guises is the bridge to Self. For women, She is the feminine part of the Self. In both genders, She is the creative matrix that gives birth to the new order."***

The Black Madonna and Her dark color represent the essence of the pure undifferentiated energy of the Universal Presence that ultimately moves the undifferentiated energy to known form. As an archetypal energy, the Black Madonna is the representation of life, death, and rebirth, the eternal cosmic movement of life.

The Black Madonna's archetypal power is that of empowerment, transformation and change. Hers is the energy that always desires to move through the individual and through humanity and to move them forward, if they are willing.

Tim Wallace-Murphy and Marilyn Hopkins, in *Rosslyn; Guardian of the Secrets of the Holy Grail*, propose that at first blush the Black Madonna looks as if she a variation on the Catholic image of the Virgin Mary, however, when one looks closely at her beginnings, they will see that she is not. Wallace-Murphy shares that the Black Madonna was brought to Europe by the Knights Templar.

The Knights Templar was a group that had a strong Egyptian influence, and in Egyptian symbolism, the color black denoted wisdom. Due to this influence, it is conjectured that the Templars were actually venerating the Mother of Wisdom, the ancient goddess Sophia, in the form of the goddess Isis with her son Horus. However, to disguise this history, the Templars gave the Black Madonna the aura of the Virgin and Child.

Another thought that Wallace-Murphy shares is that in 1128 when the Templars were drawing up plans for "Notre Dame" cathedral. Bernard of Clairvaux decreed that all Knight Templars would venerate Mary, however, instead of dedicating the churches to Mother Mary, the Templars covertly dedicated them to Mary Magdalene, who in esoteric tradition, is "the symbol of divine wisdom." In fact, some traditions depict Mary Magdalene dressed in black, like Isis, with Sophia's crown of stars surrounding her head. This picture of Mary Magdalene made me think of the description given in Revelation 12 of the woman standing on the Earth with a crown of stars above her head.

When the Black Madonna's energy is brought to awareness and there is a feeling of resonance with her, her transforming power of healing, empowerment, and love triggers a desire within us to begin the journey to the luminous darkness, a journey that ultimately brings us to a state of balance and wholeness. Be assured that when this resonance is felt, an initiation to her sacred mystery and wisdom is beginning.

She plants within our hearts a desire that beckons us to face the mystery of the energy of luminous darkness, to begin to explore the arena of the subconscious mind and the contents thereof. For when we choose to participate in Her transformation and are willing to overcome our fears and our projections, She bestows new insights on us. We discover that through the activities of nonresistance and acceptance we are blessed with inner transformation. Delving to the depths of the subconscious mind is a must if we are to go forward on our journey to finding Self.

As was mentioned earlier, often one's introduction to the feminine aspect of being begins with a dream or a vision that appears as one of the various archetypes hidden in the collective unconscious, a.k.a., race consciousness. It is common for these dreams to occur after times of stress or personal loss. The archetype emerges to consciousness, where it finds expression as a symbolic figure of the Black Madonna (Mary or one of a myriad of other goddesses or feminine nature of the Divine figures).

Working with the archetypal patterns that reside in the darkness of the collective unconscious helps us to achieve new insights to our spiritual and psychological processes. They are an essential part of our awareness that help us to illuminate our unconscious ways of behaving. As an archetypal model for self-awareness, the Black Madonna specifically provides an entryway to the deeper question of our essential identity.

An archetype is a pattern of behavior or energy that lives in the collective unconscious mind and surfaces as awareness in the conscious mind. An archetype has the ability to make us aware of our strengths and weaknesses and to mirror the emotional residue (positive and negative) that has been derived from our personal experiences, as well as the collective experience of humankind.

I personally define the word archetype as a pattern of behavior or a collection of energy that lives in the subconscious mind and that is then reflected to the conscious mind as awareness or acted out as a behavior, depending on the situation we are confronted with.

Our conscious mind is that aspect of our mind that mediates between our inner world and the outer world. The collective patterns of energies that we reflect can originate either from our personal subconscious or the collective subconscious mind.

Our personal subconscious holds our personal past memories, good and not so good. It contains the painful experiences that we have repressed or actually forgotten on purpose and perceptions that are not yet ripe for dealing with but are lurking in the shadow waiting for their opportunity to come forth.

The collective unconscious contains the collective memories that are common to all people. Carl Jung says that it is ***"the place where primordial image common to humanity lies sleeping."*** The collective unconscious is the universal projection of the collective thoughts and emotions of humankind that are contained in the underlying matrix of creation. They represent both positive and negative qualities within society as a whole, e.g., the Cinderella story, the hero's journey, the role of a victim, and the Black Madonna. Since they are archetypes that are common to the whole of society, their images can arise or emerge in mind spontaneously without our having any prior conscious knowledge of them.

Archetypes as a pattern of behavior may be either honored or dishonored depending on what the collective societal agreement has been. For example, the hero is honored and the witch is not. Yet each may show up in our dreams to teach us something about ourselves.

Archetypes as a collective energy in consciousness are alive and have the ability to trigger us emotionally. This happens because they reflect our inner state of emotional being.

We must begin to develop the capacity to comprehend archetypes, to learn to differentiate and move freely among them. Whether it is the witch, the maiden, the hero, the princess, the step mother, fool, or weak father who comes to mind, each one comes to teach us something different about our self and to provide a map for our growth as we tread the evolutionary spiral.

Archetypes tend to make their selves known to us when we are ready for a jolt of awareness concerning who we really are. They are models for self-awareness, providing an entry way to the question, "Who am I?"

As patterns of behaviors in the unconscious trying to make us aware of our strengths and weaknesses, archetypes mirror the emotional residue (positive or negative) that has come from our experiences in life and from the collective experiences of humankind. This latter statement accounts for the reason that these archetypes appear as symbols in our dreams; even when we have not ever personally ever heard of them or had an experience with them. And we can rest assured that if an archetype emerges in our life's experience, we are ready for new growth. By learning to recognize and acknowledge archetypes and our relationship with them, we learn to participate in our growth rather than fighting our way through it. This acceptance is very empowering in the overall scheme of evolutionary movement for self and the world.

It has been said that archetypes first found their way to conscious awareness through oral storytelling because the people could not write. Once there was a written form of communication, the stories were recorded as myths. The myths and stories reflected or mirrored the qualities that humankind needed to excel and grow, e.g., the quest for the Holy Grail and the Knights of the Round Table, Snow White, and Cinderella.

From these myths and others like them, we can gain insight to what negative qualities such as jealously, rivalry, greed, and unkindness can do to the fabric of a family and to humankind. From them we can glean how truth, justice, beauty, and love can triumph over the negative aspects of the human spirit.

The journey to the sacred darkness lets us learn to embrace each aspect of the One instead of running from an aspect out of fear. In order for us to awaken and grow to our full potential, the energy of any dysfunctional or negative archetype (e.g., witch, wicked stepmother) must be acknowledged or embraced in order that it may be released. This release of blocked energy (negative repressed thoughts) frees up the vital energy (positive free flowing energy waiting to be used) that is behind the negative thought.

Archetypes as patterns of behaviors are an essential part of our awareness, for they can help to illuminate our unconscious ways of behaving. These unconscious behaviors are those things that we do that we are not aware of, e.g., our family always told us that we were unlovable and didn't deserve to be loved. We were told this so often that the emotional residue of the experience became a part of our unconscious memory bank. Now as adults we find that every time we get to a relationship and it begins to feel like it may be going somewhere, we do something to ruin it. We don't know why, but it always seems to happen this way. It happens because on an unconscious level we sabotage the relationship. After all, we really don't deserve it because we are unlovable. This is called the Shadow.

The Shadow is all the unresolved issues we have lurking in the unconscious that come forth and govern our behaviors without our conscious knowledge. This makes it very difficult to heal these behaviors, for if we don't see them how can we heal them? The interesting thing about this is that other people can usually see our negative patterns and behaviors, but we refuse to. Our work is to acknowledge and give expression to these undeveloped parts of us and allow them to heal.

When we begin our work to become conscious and aware of who we are, this usually happens as a result of our being willing to look within, with total honesty, and change those behaviors that have controlled our lives in a negative way. This is very empowering and empowered people abound with energy that they use to co-create a good life. Archetypes and energy—there is a direct link between the two.

Fred Gustafson, in *The Black Madonna*, refers to the idea that the Black Madonna is an archetypal image that expresses the dark side of the feminine in a creative transformational way for both the individual and collective. This darkness is associated not with evil or negativity but with the contents of the unconscious.

A Madonna Moment

A Gift from the Black Madonna—a Meditation Experience

As we open our minds and our hearts in this time of meditation, I would ask you to give the Black Madonna, the Divine Mother, the Holy Spirit, the nurturing aspect of the feminine of the Divine permission to move through you as Love, Self-Love.

In giving your permission you are saying "yes" to the possibility of releasing the fears that are within you in order that you might heal at depth.

Life started with breath, Creation began through the breath, for Spirit is the breath of Life. Begin by taking three deep breaths. Breathe, 1—2—3, relax, relax, relax, let go and let the Divine be divine in you.

Start relaxing your body go to your feet—breath in—move up to your knees—relax hips and pelvis, your internal organs, relax every cell of your Being.

Relax your arms, then your shoulders; be willing to give up the burdens of the universe. Relax your neck, your head; allow your mind to take you deeper, interiorly. Let the breath of the Holy Spirit bring new life to you; let Her relax you. Know the truth that "I of myself can do nothing."

Now using the power of your imagination, imagine that there is a cave directly in front of you. The large opening beckons you to come closer. If you have been afraid of dark places, accept that fear and continue to walk towards the opening.

This cave represents the womb of the Divine Mother. She is beckoning you to come deeper into Her Mystery and learn more of who you are. As you enter the cave and its darkness, let your intention be to be open to finding out more about who you are as the Feminine nature of the Divine. Give yourself permission to be one with this Feminine Energy of the Universe that lives within your being.

At the entrance to the cave is a set of steps, you can see them clearly through the darkness. You are going to descend nine steps, with each step you will go deeper down into the cave, the womb of Mother-Earth and the Divine Mother.

As you take your first step, consciously focus on your breath. Be open and receptive to all the gifts that the Divine Mother has in store for you through this meditation experience.

As you descend to the second step, begin to release any past experience of unloving thoughts, words or actions directed at you by others. Ask your heart if there is someone you are ready to forgive. Allow his or her face to come to view and silently acknowledge that you are letting him or her go, that you are freeing that person from the confines of your mental prison.

As a child of the Divine you no longer need to hold onto that which is not the highest and best for you. Let go of the pain, the hurt of the previous moments of life. Breathe.

Taking the third step is about forgiving yourself. The Divine Mother loves you and forgives you for all thoughts, words, and actions that you have put out against others.

In taking the fourth step, the Divine Mother opens your heart and allows you to see that every person in your life has been there as a teacher, a gift to teach you more about who you are. All were brought to you in order that you might grow into who you are in this very moment.

With step five you begin to feel a sense of lightness within your heart-space. Your heart is open to the Love that desires to be birthed through you. Regardless of what your experiences and/or feelings may be towards your earthly mother/caregiver, send a thought of love or kindness towards her. If you are willing, tell her that you love her in the consciousness of unconditional Love. Picture her face clearly, look into her eyes and listen, as she looks at you and says, "I love you my child." Be open to having her share these words with you.

Next, regardless of what your experiences and/or feelings may be to towards your earthly father/caregiver, send a thought of love or kindness towards him. If you are willing, tell him that you love him in the consciousness of unconditional Love. Look into his eyes and listen, as he looks at you and says, "I love you my child." Be open to having him share these words with you.

The sixth step brings a sense of renewal and acceptance. As you forgive, you are open and receptive to acceptance, self- acceptance. You accept who you are, exactly as you are.

Taking the seventh step, you open to your I AM power. I am statements come streaming forth; "I Am free from the burdens of the past." "I Am free fromthe need to be loved by everyone." "I Am love." "I love myself." "I Am worthy of love."

With the eighth step a veil is removed and you are more clearly able to see yourself as the divine feminine. What do you see? How are you different?

On stepping onto the ninth step, you are now standing in the midst of darkness and you feel the Divine surrounding you. In front of you is Golden White Blazing Light and it is moving towards you. In the midst of the Light is a feminine figure. In her hands, is a gift especially for you – and it is only for you. She offers the gift to you. Now you must decide if you will take it? If you are ready to accept Her gifts, stretch forth your hand and allow Her to place it in the palm of your hand.

If you accept the gift, before you look to see what it is—know that whatever She has given you has come to invite you to walk through a doorway to something greater within yourself. Therefore, do not discount or negate anything that you see or that comes to mind. Now using the power of imagination, feel the shape of the gift in your hand. Does it emit any energy? If so, what does it feel like?

Again, with your mind's eye, look at the gift. What is it? What does it represent for your life? If you do not know, ask your Inner Feminine what the gift represents for you. Now, ask the gift what special message you are to take from it, back into the world.

Thank the Divine Feminine (the Black Madonna, the Divine Mother, the El Shaddai, the Holy Spirit) for revealing Herself and Her gift to you. Thank Her for Her love that flows through you.

Before you turn to ascend the staircase, take your gift and place it over your heart-space. Let it imbue itself into your being. As you begin to ascend the stairway with your gift, know that with each step you ascend, the gift will absorb itself deeper to your being. 9 – 8 –7, 6—5—4, deeper into your cellular system the gift makes it way. 3—2—1, you and the gift are one.

As you step into the light of day and step forth to go out into the world, go forward knowing that the gift is there waiting to be shared with the world.

When you are ready, slowly and gently open your eyes. Bring your attention to this moment and re-enter the space of your body.

Amen.

PART I

ENTERING LUMINOUS DARKNESS

"Darkness is nature's time of rest, formation, incubation and secret rendezvous of invisible powers and unseen realities."
—Rocco Errico: *Treasures from the Language of Jesus*

"Descent to the unconscious involves abandoning the ego's clamor in order to come to contact with one's deeper psyche, whose goal is wholeness."
—Fred Gustafson: *The Black Madonna*

"Darkness within darkness, the gateway to all understanding."
—Lao Tzu

CHAPTER 1

EMBRACING LUMINOUS DARKNESS IS 'THE GATEWAY TO ALL UNDERSTANDING'

Darkness—Unmanifested Universal Energy

"In the beginning...the Earth was without form and void, and darkness was on the face of the deep."
—Genesis 1: *The Christian Testament*, RSV

Darkness, unformed matter, universal energy in its undifferentiated state, waits and desires to be called forth to expression by the ***Light***. The energy of ***Darkness*** is intense, powerful, full of mystery, and holds many untold wonders.

"Black, or the state of darkness, is not a curse, nor is it evil...
Darkness holds many hidden wonders.
In the blackness of the night, stars are seen.
In the darkness of the womb, life is conceived.
In the darkness of the soil, seeds germinate.
In the darkness of the inner mind, ideas are born."
—Rocco Errico: *Treasures from the Language of Jesus*

Darkness, the creative, swirling, unformed, universal energy in its undifferentiated state, holds many mysteries. Jean Shinoda Bolen, teacher and educator on women's mysteries, speaks of having entered the darkness and returning as ***endarkenment.*** She refers to *endarkenment* as the wisdom that is gained from having gone to the darkness and come out again. According to Bolen, there are times when we must enter the darkness in order to grow. Life is not linear; it is a circular, spiral course, a movement of light and dark.

This spiral course ultimately leads to the experience of Integrative Spirituality, which is the reintegration to consciousness of both the darkness and the light; the subconscious and conscious minds; the masculine and feminine aspects of being.

Is it Darkness versus Light?

Luminous darkness holds the space for the hallowed interplay of the dance of the Great Paradox, which results in the conscious and unconscious minds working together to create an alchemical transformation of one's total being. Evolvement of consciousness requires learning to dance within the spaciousness of the paradoxes, learning to recognize all the various forms and disguises that each paradox takes on,

\

disguises that try to keep us enmeshed in the appearance of separateness.

Sacred interplay creates the space for the possibility of a harmonic resonance that will call forth our greatest potential and creative possibility. Also occurring when the opposites are given the opportunity to move and sway is a natural state of harmony and balance. Albeit, it may only last for a brief moment before they separate again. The willingness to explore the depths of the sacred darkness gives us the opportunity to dance the dance of dynamic opposites with Grace. When the exploration of the dance of the paradox becomes the accepted norm of human society what we will discover is that "opposites are complementary, not contradictory."

As we are willing to journey to the luminous darkness of consciousness, we have the opportunity to come to contact with those fragmented aspects of our selves that we have in the past disowned or not recognized—aspects that, once discovered and uncovered, we can begin to reclaim—reclaim in order that we might live consciously in a state of wholeness.

If we desire deeply in our hearts to know the fullness of the Universal Presence, then we must be willing to know It in all its aspects—including the Light and the Darkness. Both are part of The One. We cannot love one and fear the other; we must respect them both for what they bring to the table of awareness.

Light represents those qualities of God that we know about intellectually: God as Peace, God as Love, God as Joy, But we only know these Light qualities as concepts that we have interpreted from our relative and limited human understanding of them. We have given these qualities a spin according to how we have seen them play out in our lives.

Darkness as an aspect of God is that which we can only know from our intuitive, feeling nature. Inherent within darkness is the creative movement and chaos that lives in the realm of the unknown. It is this creative movement of the Unknown that calls forth the known to manifestation. The luminous darkness contains the Mystery of God; it is God as the Hidden Power, the Unknowable, and the Creative Force.

If we are ever to become comfortable with and in the Mystery of the Unknown, we must be willing to accept that darkness exists and that it also has inherent good contained within. If darkness has such a wide range of symbolic meaning, then why is it that "we" as a collective society have chosen to only reflect on what has been labeled the negative aspect of darkness? For if one desires to know the Truth, then one must be willing to know Truth in all of Its aspects—Light and Darkness.

There are many creation stories from various religions that reflect the power of darkness and the mystery of the Unknown and the Unknowable. They are beautiful expressions of the dance of Oneness, the movement between light and darkness.

In the ***Hindu Vedas*** we find these words:

In the beginning, darkness lay wrapped in darkness;
All was one undifferentiated sea
Then, within that one undifferentiated Existence,
{Something} arose by the heat of concentrated energy.
What arose in That, in the beginning, was Desire,
{Which is} the primal seed of mind.
The wise, having searched deep within their own hearts,
Have perceived the bond between the Real and the unreal.

In the "***Tao Teh Ching,***" Lao Tzu shares:

Before heaven and Earth existed,
there was something unformed, silent, alone,
unchanging, constant and eternal;
It could be called "the Source of the Universe,"
I do not know Its name and simply call It—Tao....
The Tao that can be spoken of is not the absolute Tao.
The Nameless {Tao} is the Father of heaven and Earth;
that which is named {Teh} is the Mother of all things.
These two are the same; they are given different names
in order to distinguish between them.
Together they constitute the Supreme Mystery.

Sir Wallis Budge shares in ***Gods of the Egyptians***:

***"There was a time when neither heaven nor Earth existed
and when nothing had being except the boundless primeval water,
which was however, shrouded with thick darkness.
In this condition, the primeval water remained for a considerable time,
not withstanding that it contained within it germs of the things which afterwards came to existence in this world and the world itself.
At length, the Spirit of the primeval water felt the desire for creative activity,
and having uttered the word, the world sprang straightway to being
in the form which had already been depicted in the mind of the Spirit
before he spake the word which resulted in its creation."***

In the Western tradition, we find that in both the Hebrew (Old) Testament and the Christian (New) Testament there are accounts and/or references to God as darkness, none of which has a negative connotation. Each scripture describes God as a positive reflection of the mystery of darkness and the paradoxical relationship of light and darkness.

Genesis 1:2 "***The Earth was without form and void, and darkness was on the face of the deep; and the Spirit of God was moving over the face of the waters.***"

What was going on here in this scene of darkness and chaos? It would appear that only darkness existed. Yet this blackness seemed to contain a creative life force that was making itself known by moving on the face of the deep, the waters, brooding, in a churning black chaos. In the midst of the darkness, which seemed like nothingness, there was a creative intelligence desiring to project Itself. The Holy Spirit moved over the chaotic dark energy of unformed matter getting it ready for movement to form, matter and light. And it did!

Perhaps this is the same thing that happens when we are in the midst of change. What appears as a "dark" time is actually the Holy Spirit brooding, waiting for us to allow the light to come through and create something new.

Genesis 1:3–5 finds God creating day and night. ***"And God said, 'Let there be light'; and there was light. And God saw that the light was good; and God separated the light from the darkness."***

There is an interesting thought to note here. Light was created from darkness, therefore, there is never a time when darkness did not exist. How did we move from *darkness* having a special and sacred meaning, as a place where creative action takes place, birthing begins, and a void that contains all potential power, to darkness as evil, fear, and negativity?

An answer lies in the word *Unknown*. When the ego-conscious mind began to take control, reason and logic demanded to know the answers to all that was labeled *Known*. The unknown, the unexplainable was relegated to a place of dishonor because how can an intelligent person explain the unexplainable? Therefore, rather than having to deal with the unknown, it was ignored, shut away, deemed unimportant. From that ignoring and repression, a fear developed around darkness and anything associated with it, e.g., the night, the color black, cave, womb, and evil.

Exodus 19:9, 16 The Lord is telling Moses how He will reveal Himself. ***"And the Lord said to Moses, 'Lo, I am coming to you in a thick [dark] cloud, that the people may hear when I speak with you, and may also believe you forever...On the morning of the third day there was thunder and lightning and a thick [dark] cloud."*** From the darkness God spoke to Moses in order that the people might believe his words. The mystery is of God's revealing Itself in a paradox, expressing Itself as both the known {God's voice heard on Earth} and the unknown {shrouded in darkness, unable to be seen}.

Psalm 18:6–11 Another example of the paradoxical nature of God's revealing Itself in both the light and darkness is in Psalm 18:6–11. Here God is helping David in a time of distress. ***"To my God I cried for help...My cry to him reached his ears...He bowed the heavens and came down...He [God] made darkness his covering around him."***

Psalms 139:12 may be the most profound description of God and darkness.

"For darkness is as light to Thee." Here David is using the word *darkness* to describe the chaos he is in the midst of. Yet even in the midst of turmoil, there is no fear of this kind of "darkness" in his statement. For David understands that God is in the midst of darkness and yet can see all things in a "perfect state."

Let us look at a seed as an example of this "perfect state" at work. When a seed is planted in the darkness of the womb of Earth, it begins to gather energy from an invisible source until the seed finally breaks open. On the opening or "awakening" the seed begins its journey toward the fulfillment of its potential. The seed doesn't complain that its path is too hard, that the journey wasn't what the seed thought it might be. It breaks open in the glory of the darkness in order to grow and unfold. Once opened, it patiently waits, gathering the essence of the creative life force, waiting until it has accepted all that the darkness has to give and is finally able to break through to the light. Could it be that this metaphor is related in some way to our lives here on Earth?

This same thing happens with a thought. We receive an energetic thought-form out of the darkness of the unknown, the undifferentiated substance of the ethers. This thought-form enters the darkness of our mind, the unconscious mind, and stirs around in the mind until we have collected enough thought-energy for it to be called forth to the light of conscious mind. Even within the conscious mind, a thought, in order to be made manifest, must continue to draw energy from the unknown.

Could it be that we have been deluded by what we believe to be or have labeled as light, good, dark, bad, and evil? Perhaps we have it backwards. What if this life on Earth is the soil and we are actually in darkness that we have labeled as light? We (humankind) as individuals are the "seeds" awaiting our awakening or breaking open in order that we might begin to gather the essence of the creative life force and eventually fulfill our potential, entering the true Light.

As was stated previously, the journey to the luminous darkness is a metaphor for the process that occurs as we reintegrate the darkness and the light, the unconscious and conscious minds. This reclamation process for many individuals begins on the archetypal level, which is alive in the luminous darkness of the subconscious mind.

Befriending the Subconscious Realm

"Having forgotten who we are as spiritual beings
Has entrenched us in the mire of materiality,
Turning within and touching that place of Silence
Returns us to remembrance."
—T.G.B.

Luminous darkness as a metaphor for the spiritual journey and the transformative process leads us to the uncovering of the hidden *Wisdom* that lies within the depths of our being. However, in order for this Imprisoned *Wisdom* to be released, there must first be a "clean-up" in consciousness undertaken.

Initially, the conscious mind must be prepared so that the deeper work which comes later (subconscious mind work), can be successful. Ultimately, what we are striving towards is the harmonious working of the conscious and subconscious minds which opens the way for the Higher Self (a.k.a., Higher Power, Spirit, Superconscious Mind, God), to be *That* which is in "control" of our lives.

As was referred to, as we embark on the spiritual path, the first "clean-up work cycle" begins in the realm of the conscious mind. The conscious mind is that aspect of mind that keeps us connected to the physical plane through our five senses (taste, touch, hearing, seeing, and smell). The conscious mind, looks around and utilizes the information that it gathers from the input received from the senses and then determines if what it thinks or feels needs to be changed based upon the input.

When we start the spiritual "clean up," we begin to take charge of the thoughts of the conscious mind. Through the conscious use of affirmations and denials, forgiveness work, prayer, and so forth, we forge ahead with this "clean-up work." In this phase, however, we are "in charge," we decide what aspects of our lives need to be changed or shifted and we go for it.

After the conscious mind has been prepared, which may take years, the next phase of the spiritual journey is initiated. The activity in this stage occurs through the realm of the subconscious mind. However, in this phase, we are not truly in control of the "work."

Because of the years of preparation that it takes to reach this stage, there is, by this time, a spiritual energy moving in and through us that guides this portion of the journey. The deeper work that is done in the subconscious arena initiates a movement of energy, which draws forth the dreams, archetypes, and symbols that are a part of the healing process which occurs in this phase of the journey.

Unlike conscious-mind work, which is driven by an overt desire to change some aspect of our lives, work in the subconscious mind is more of a covert activity. We cannot necessarily direct the activities of healing and transformation taking place here. The conscious work demanded at this juncture, is to surrender to the activities of Spirit as It moves through to call forth the next phase of healing.

Working within the realm of the darkness of the subconscious mind calls forth the shadows that lurk within. These "shadows" are made up of the remnants of the memories of our past experiences, emotions, and beliefs that have coagulated into an energetic block. It is this congealed shadow-stuff which actually creates the sense of separation from God that we experience, but do not understand. In this phase of the work, these remnants are called forth from their hiding places and brought into the light of conscious awareness. Full participation in this aspect of the journey ultimately leads to the unveiling of the hidden *Wisdom* contained within (sometimes referred as the, *Imprisoned Splendor*).

This hidden *Wisdom*, reveals that there are no opposites in consciousness, only complements. Complements which are in a continual dance between the so-called paradoxes of life. Paradoxes or opposites like masculine/feminine, good/bad, dark/light, , are not meant to be held in an either/or static state. What happens when we are forced to make a choice between the opposites, especially when we proclaim that one is good and the other is bad, is that the aspect that is not chosen tends to get denied, discounted, cut off, dismissed, submerged, or repressed. Thus, life goes into a state of in-harmony or unbalance and we wonder how it happened.

When paradoxes are seen as complements, instead of opposites, there is a new dynamic set up and ultimately life becomes less of a struggle. When we allow room for the "dance of the complements" in consciousness, spaciousness is created, and we are not confined to one way versus another. We stay open to the gifts that each aspect has to offer, because both aspects remain honored and respected. This integration (versus separation) of the complements—darkness and light; masculine and feminine natures of the Divine; conscious and subconscious minds; transcendent and immanent; spirit and body; and so on—allows us to view life differently and ultimately moves us to a new levels of awareness.

"Will, desire, pain, and anguish are the raw materials
through which something powerful and mighty is brought to pass.
God is love, to be sure, but love is...a process
whose eternal, hidden building blocks are in desire, pain and anguish.
Thus these things are not to be feared or denied...
but transformed."
—Cynthia Bourgeault: *Gnosis* magazine, fall 1997

As was stated, for full spiritual development to occur, we must be willing to meet and experience the shadows lurking within the subconscious mind. It is through this meeting that we learn to recognize the superficial responses of the "adverse" ego and call forth the true essence of our being. We must face those adverse aspects of ourselves that show up as jealousy, greed, control, manipulation, or "my way." Those aspects of our personality that we have used as coping mechanisms in order to survive (because we did not know any better) must be acknowledged and accepted as part of who we are before any growth can take place. These are the ego parts of us that are still attached to having things our way.

When we begin to look at our lives and our values asking, "Who am I?" we start to assess our depth of being and the strength of our ego. When this happens, the ego will fight to keep its place of honor. The world tells us to be greedy. It tells us that "me first" is a perfectly okay response. After all, how else would we gain anything? In being willing to enter the darkness and confronting the shadow aspects of self (greed, guilt, jealousy), we actually find the dark strength of the unconscious. For this transformation to take place, the old must die to a new way of being.

This death takes a total willingness to surrender and change at depth. In this "death" we find new life. The conscious mind, with its attachment to the outer world, materialism, and perceived ego needs, believes that the dark, destroying elements of the unconscious are evil, wrong, frightening, and bad. However, transformation of consciousness cannot occur without giving up old beliefs and ways of being and adopting new attitudes and beliefs.

This is very frightening to the ego. The ego enjoys status quo, even if it involves suffering and pain because at least they are familiar and the ego is comfortable in the familiar. This unknown is scary territory.

The unconscious, like the siren's call, beckons us to enter its uncharted wilderness. Once we enter, we find that it acts in one of two ways. The first is a provider of wisdom and insights, insights that initiate healing if we choose to stay conscious. The second has the power to take us in another direction. It can scatter and destroy us or pull us in multiple directions if we do not have the inner strength or support systems in place to keep us centered. It is through bringing forth the contents of the unconscious and desiring to "dance" with them, rather than keeping them submerged and hidden, that we truly begin to develop wholeness and balance.

For instance, the subconscious arena is considered by many as the playground of the energies of the archetypal feminine and "She" knows that our shadows must and can only be transformed by, with and through Love. Therefore, as we willingly integrate the energies of the feminine into our conscious awareness, we are moved back to proper relationship with Earth, self, and all of life—all matter.

Being in relationship with matter is something that our masculine-dominated thought has shifted us away from. The Mother–Mater calls us back to it. She represents the bounty and wisdom of being in relationship with matter. (Remember, when a person is in the deep, honest, communion of relationship, he or she does not tend to use or destroy that with which he or she is in relationship with. Just the opposite, the person tends to honor and guard it as a precious jewel.)

Everyone has a shadow-side; none of us are alone in this. Willingly participating in shadow-work is in part learning to unify the opposites that live within us, coming to see all the polarities that exist within our lives and the universe. Through doing our inner work, examining all aspects of our being and making them conscious, we come to find that it is the sense of separation that we carry about these polarities that keep us out of a consciousness of wholeness, of recognizing ourselves as sacred-humans.

Seeing the polarities of the world as one is better than the other, causes us to want to reject and suppress the "bad" one, rather than seeing each of them as two aspects of who we are. Much of the sense of fragmentation in life is caused by wearing "masks" that are intended to cover those polar opposites that we have repressed or rejected. But yet, much still exists within us in the depths of our subconscious minds. True Self-discovery begins when we are willing to ask the questions of, "Who am I?" or "What is the opposite trait of who I am being right now?" Being willing to query takes us to another dimension of our selves and can surprise the heck out of us, also.

To create a truly great life, we must reclaim both sides of the polarities that reside within our beings and begin to see them as complements. However, this can only happen when we are willing to move to a consciousness of being self-aware. Self-awareness is the prelude to awakening to a Higher Consciousness and NO ONE can ripen in spiritual maturity without it.

Let us shift our attention for a moment to a metaphor that will help to explain much of what we have just discussed. The metaphor is that of a diamond's inner brilliance. A diamond comes in many shapes and sizes, none any better than the other, just a little bigger or smaller, depending on what the buyer is looking for. However, regardless of the size, to shine brightly, each diamond must be thoroughly cleaned and then shaped with precision by a master. Therefore, in order for the diamond to shine brightly there is an orderly process that the diamond must go through to uncover the inner brilliance. This same metaphor applies to each of us.

When we are willing to befriend the unconscious realm, we are saying yes to uncover another facet of our brilliance. Wiping away the "murk" hidden in the luminous darkness allows us to be a clearer reflection for the glory of the One to shine through. If this idea holds truth then perhaps the "darkest" times of our lives are actually cleansing experiences meant to allow our inner brilliance to shine a little brighter. This would then make those "tough" growth periods the master diamond cutter or teacher whose work it is to shape our spiritual lives.

The archetypal feminine, whether in the form of the Black Madonna or another form, could be thought of as the master diamond cutters and teachers. For when they are encountered, whether it is through a dream or an introduction of another kind—they begin to make their presence known through desiring to teach us about our Inner Glory. They reveal themselves through our experiences, in whatever form of the birth, death, rebirth, or "shaping" cycle we need in the moment. Their ultimate goal, regardless of appearance, is that of helping us to shine more brightly, to come forth In-lightened.

People tend to fear the subconscious mind and project the idea that all that it contains is negative and destructive. Entering to the subconscious realm takes us to the path of returning to the knowledge of our oneness and multi-dimensionality, but we must develop a willingness to unveil the contents of the subconscious if we are to return to all that is. It is the archetypal Feminine that helps birth that willingness.

Until we willingly enter the subconscious realm, we will and cannot discover the vast reservoir of understanding, the hidden treasures, pearls of wisdom and a multitude of skills that we were not aware that we had. These and more are the gifts that we have access to once we begin to take the journey inward.

Some people may ask, "Why is the spiritual journey important? Why do we need to return "Home?" Why do we need to participate in subconscious work?" In esoteric circles, it is said that the body is the out-picturing of soul and the soul dwells within the One Great Mind and the connection to this One Mind is made through the subconscious mind.

However, through attachments to things of this earthly plane, we have forgotten our connection to the One Mind and have created false beliefs that have resulted in a belief in separateness, from one another and from the One. And all of these false beliefs have taken up residence in the subconscious mind.

The journey Home through the path of the subconscious mind helps us to remove the blocks, attachments, illusions, and false beliefs that we have created about separation and brings us back to the full awareness of the Truth of who we are. For me this journey Home has been and continues to be aided by the archetypes of the Feminine nature, all of which live in the collective unconscious, which is contained within the subconscious mind.

As you can see, the subconscious mind is a repository. It does not know the difference between right and wrong, for as a repository it houses everything that is put into it. It contains the Truth of the One (our innate Divinity) and the "junk" we continually feed it through our lower thoughts and emotions. Thus our work becomes that of clearing out the junk in order that the Truth may shine forth.

For many, the first encounter of meeting the dark-skinned Madonna comes right before a tough life experience or in the midst of pain, turmoil, anguish, or illness. It seems that She shows up during times of strife because often we are not open to learning our lessons when things are going well.

She appears for She desires to guide us to a higher purpose and realization, teaching us to see the sacredness and beauty in the moment, regardless of its appearance, giving us the strength and courage to face, honor, and overcome our deepest fears. She teaches us to work with life in new ways. For some She teaches that anger can be a tool to use in order to begin to learn to say no and to come more to a sense of who they are. Others learn that anger should not be used to control, manipulate, or bully situations and people.

But most of all, She teaches each of us how to have a relationship with our self. Honesty and authenticity become the pillars of our existence. Learning how to honestly communicate our wants and desires becomes of utmost importance. Honesty of thought, word and deed are the underlying activities of being authentic in every situation.

The Feminine aspect of self grinds away at the grit and dirt hidden in the subconscious mind and teaches us the great lesson of "To thine own self be true." Inherent in this lesson is the recognition that we are not "Stepford Wife" look-alikes. (A "Stepford wife" is an expression from a movie, that describes the willlingness of a person to forego their own sense of self and to live by someone else's notion of how they should look or act. In other words, they submit to a life that is under the control of another person.). Our work is to learn to glean the essence of who we are as individuals, as our own person, and then to live authentically from that truth; to allow our Light to shine brightly, through the prisms of our Being, unimpeded. The Black Madonna is one of the archetypes that take us from being children of the world to being spiritually mature.

Out of this new sense of relationship with Self and the deeper revelation of "who I am," emerges a knowing that begins to reveal one's life mission—the work we are called to do by the universe—not have to do just in order to make money.

By opening to the mystery of the unconscious realm, we begin to perceive that we are much more than we ever dreamed we were. We can learn to delve into its mystery and explore it as a part of who we are. In the rich darkness of the unconscious we have an opportunity to explore every aspect of our self and to unlock our hidden potential, to let the inner diamond shine. The truth is that through the exploration of the unconscious mind we are offered the greatest opportunities for awakening. By venturing inward and shining the light of truth on what we find there, we will begin to change. This transformation occurs, not through resistance but through persistence.

There is an old adage that says, "**What we resist persists.**" So, enter into those moments of life that "force" you to look at yourself—full of expectation. Experience the range of emotions you find in there. Get to know and understand yourself as guilt, fear, rage, anger, jealousy, covetousness, pride, self-righteousness, poor me, and yes, even joy.

A Madonna Moment

"Often an awareness of the divine Feminine or an interest in the idea of learning to live in the world from the wisdom of the heart is a signal that the psyche is prepared for a purification process that will ultimately conceive the newborn Self. The purification process or "burning" begins to rend the shadow sides of the personality, the veils of illusion, that have been used to conceal the ancient indigenous wisdom of the soul. Once manifested, the Dark Feminine wisdom will birth an understanding and awareness of the fullness of the Truth of who one is at their deepest core. This is so because Integrative Spirituality expresses the wisdom behind any notion of the Black Madonna."[5]

"Inherent in the qualities of the archetypal feminine is the ability
to light blazing fires of change, to move status quo and to bring
death to the old in order that new may be birthed.
However, these transformations do not come without a price.
The question is; "Are you willing to pay it?"
—T.G.B.

The Black Madonna was and is an ally and a teacher who came to tutor me about the more important things of life. Over the years She has blessed me with a deeper understanding of who I am as a spiritual being and has taught me how to live from my Center-point. This is my experience, in story form, of what happens when one journeys into and begins to befriend the elements "living" in the luminous darkness of the subconscious/unconscious realm.

"I was introduced to the concept of the Black Madonna in the early 1990's. The moment Her name was mentioned to me, my heart leapt. I went on a search to find out more about Her and what it was that She had to offer me. At first, it was a purely intellectual pursuit. I read everything I could find about Her. I reflected on these findings and placed pictures of Her on my altar. I questioned Her reality. "Who are you?" I lamented. "I feel you have something to teach me. What is it?"

On August 4th, 1996, the Black Madonna whispered the following words to me.:

"We are One, You and I, not two but One.
Remember Me. Return to Me.
Let Me strip away all that is not who you are.
Be willing to be vulnerable,
Let Me lift the veils of illusion from your eyes,
For I have come to awaken you to the depths of your hidden glory."
T.G.B.

In a flash, She changed from a concept to a "living reality." The spark of fire that I had been tending in my heart, became a flame, and I was ignited – never to be the same again. From this heart-filled experience, She began to pour Herself through me in the forms of poems, articles, plays, songs, and more. Consciously, I had never considered myself a creative individual. I had thought, rather, that my skills were more of an administrative character. Now, however, She was soon to turn my world inside-out and upside-down.

From the moment that Her flame began to blaze within my heart, life took on a whole new expression. Unbeknownst to me, not only were my creative juices flowing, but I was also being prepared to be "burnt" in Her sacred fires. With each of the "burning-experiences" that She graciously brought to me, I was changed at depth, and simultaneously a new layer of Truth about myself was revealed to me. At the end of one of these "burning experiences," I wrote imaginatively about entering the realm of the Black Madonna. It came as follows:

At First

At first, I thought that the journey into this realm, the sub-conscious mind, the Black Madonna's playground, would be fun. I thought it would provide a new thrill of traversing unknown territory and uncharted courses within my being. "Who would be afraid to look at themselves?" I piously inquired. "I will go into your hinter land", I announced smugly. "Take me, I am yours!"

The Black Madonna smiled, took my hand and said, "Come hither then, my sister." Oh, what surprises She had hidden in the depths of the darkness of my unconscious mind. I knew that the underworld of the unconscious was not a territory for one to traverse alone if one is weak of heart, but I knew that I was strong. After all, I was a "power-woman," a "rock" for those around me. I could be counted on.

Dark-skinned Wise Women, members of the Black Madonna's troupe, awaited my arrival as I began to take the first steps into their homeland. Kali, Hecate, Isis, Mary Magdalene, and others, each one, stood waiting in the wings for their turn to share their graces and gifts with me.

How they must have chuckled, for they knew what I would meet as I smugly took my first steps into their sacred terrain. I can hear them now, saying, "She thinks that she understands. She thinks that she is ready. Well, let us help her see who she really is."

Into the darkness I went, arms open. "Here I am. Show me my stuff!" Little did I know how those words would reverberate throughout the universe and be returned to me heaped up, pressed down and over-flowing with my own negative thoughts and emotions and uncomplimentary feelings about myself.

Into the dark, hidden recesses of my mind I went guided by those Dark-skinned Wise Women. They introduced me to new aspects of myself, picture after picture. Like reels of film produced just for me, they revealed how I was living life. I saw how my ego had subtlty tricked me into believing that my actions were for the "greater good" or for the good of others when, in reality, they were for my own enhancement and aggrandizement.

Feeling like I always had to be the one in control, being Miss Efficiency, always looking good, feeling self-righteousness, taking no time to rest because "they" needed. me were just a few of the tricks my ego had used to divert me from my true purpose.

That Trickster, the adverse ego, had successfully woven a web of subtle distractions. I was drawn into the web of material attachment, attached unknowingly to the glory that my so-called "success" appeared to bring.

Before me, the Black Madonnas, the Wise Dark Ones, paraded all my "attachments" and "dependencies" for my review. I was stricken with grief and screamed, "No! No! This can't be me! Honestly I have worked my stuff. I'm good. We must be in someone else's dark inner world." I cried like a baby as I saw all the shadow areas that still lived within me.

As each layer of thick, sticky, murky memories, negative beliefs, hidden emotions and old, worn-out thoughts were uncovered, waves of anguish undulated throughout my body. "How could this be? I thought I was so far along the path. After years of study and living Truth Principles, this is what I have to show for it?" The realization stabbed at me like a hot poker branding a little calf.

I realized that my ego had subtly built me a faulty pedestal upon which I had installed myself. Now it was crumbling and I was crashing to the ground. Sadness filled me. Tears exploded from my eyes like pellets from a shotgun. Deeper and deeper I spiraled into the abyss of sadness. I felt sadness as I realized how shallow my foundation had been. I grieved for who I thought I was and all the sky-castles I had built. I felt despair because I was afraid it was too late to start over.

These thoughts and emotions consumed me. They tugged at me like a child desperate to be held and would not let go. I spiraled inward, deeper than I had ever ventured to go before. Outwardly, I felt like I was a walking shell. The smug girl in me was gone and, in her place, was one whom I nick-named, "She Who Cries Easily."

I knew I had to grieve the loss of the "girl" or the "insecure one," in order that the Wise Woman be born through me. So, cry I did—at home, at work, in meetings, at lunch, talking to my grandchildren on the telephone, etc.

There was no place where tears were not permitted. Besides, I had no choice; the tears were part of the purification and cleansing process. Through this experience, I learned to honor the liquid droplets and to honor my feelings as well.

The stark awareness of my "stupidity" blinded me. For such a long time, I had put my feelings and needs aside so that I could be strong and ready to serve when others beckoned. But this was my time, and it felt good in a painful sort of way.

For weeks I lived like this, immersed in the tension as a myriad of feelings welled up inside of me. As I began to trust my feelings, I began to desire to get to know them and to recognize what it was that they had come to teach me. Gradually, I understood that I had to make friends with them. I knew that "what you resist persists," so I stopped resisting. I surrendered to the experience.

I did not know my destination, but I knew I was learning. I learned more deeply about my own boundaries, i.e., how to say, "No" to my control freak and "Yes" to taking care of myself.

My doctor had told me that I could be nominated or, better yet that I had attained full- status membership in the "Overachiever Women's Syndrome Club." Oh, how I had laughed when he had said that. Now, looking back over my life, I ponder how true this statement was. I was always trying to prove how good and efficient I was, how I could be counted on. I was not like some of the men who had been in my early life, men who left me to fend for myself, and neither was I like the one who had "hurt" me when I was ten. No, I was not like them. I could be counted on. Suddenly, I realized that this was what I had unconsciously chosen to prove to myself and to the world, namely, that I was willing to be accountable for everything and everyone whether it was required of me or not.

In this state of hurt, my outer wrappings of success, confidence, being a good girl and more started to come undone. In many ways, these facades had been holding me together, but now it was time to live from another level of awareness.

This shift in consciousness did not happen slowly. Rather, it erupted like a volcanic explosion of awareness. Here were revealed all the tears and lack of energy I felt. They were a part of the release of the pent-up pressure. It was a relief to cast off the outer wrapping. In the uncovering, I discovered that I was free. I was free to be a new version of the real me.

No longer having to be in control of the world, I now invite all of the Black Madonnas and their gifts of the mystery of life and of the unknown to eat at my table and to be my constant companions. From the depths of my heart, I have learned to call forth unconditional Love and to extend it to all I meet. I am no longer afraid of what will happen if I am not orchestrating the band. The depths of the darkness of the subconscious felt cold at first, but it was only because the false coverings, my "old ego friends", that I had been wearing and living really did not provide as much "warmth" as I thought they would.

What I now know is that the ***"spiritual path is a dynamic energy that comes from beyond and prepares us for the sacrifice of our own soul."*** It is a sacrifice that is ultimately a small price to pay for what I received, namely, freedom from the imprisonment of the illusion that I had created about who I thought I was. What I gained was the Truth about my deeper self. I learned about the importance of the dance of the opposites and how to view them in the everyday experiences of life.

What a smug girl I was when I willingly entered the sacred abyss of the unconscious mind, the initiatory playground of the Black Madonna and Her Wise

Women! What I found upon my return was that through Her willingness to love me enough and to help me peel away the illusions and the facades about who I thought I was, I found the Truth of who I really am! I recognized my imprisoned splendor and I released it! I found Freedom!" [6]

We Are Sitting at a Cosmic Crossroad, Which Way Will We Choose to Turn?

In doing research for this book, I came across several articles and chapters in books that seemed to have a synergistic energy. These writings came from the following authors; Charles Fillmore, Peter Russell, Valentine Tomberg, and Rudolph Steiner. When I contemplated the relationship of their ideas as a whole, questions arose from the depths of my being. Each question stirred something within my soul and caused another question to arise. Questions such as; "What is the purpose of life." "What is Truth?" What is the divine nature and relationship of all things?" Who am I, truly?" "What part do I play in the universal plan?" and the primary question was and still is; "We (humankind) are sitting at a cosmic crossroad, which way will we choose to turn?"

It was Peter Russell, in his book, *The White Hole of Time,* who set forth a question that caused me to consider the future of humankind and the role that we each play (individually and collectively) in the evolutionary process. His question was;

"Tomorrow's world will...be changing even faster. And beyond that yet faster still. But—where are we going? Where will our burgeoning creativity take us next?"

Sitting in the mystery of that question, other questions began to take form. "Where are we going" and "Where are we going so quickly?" I felt that the answer to these queries would lie within the decisions that humankind would make over the next few decades—decisions that would be made on both an individual and a collective level.

Furthermore, if the evolutionary future is to based on the decisions that we, the collective whole known as humankind, are making now—and I believe they are—then humankind is sitting at a cosmic crossroad in our evolutionary process. A crossroad, as a symbol, signifies possibility and the ability to choose. It is possible that through our collective decision-making process, humankind can choose to move in a new direction and as a species we can evolve to a new level of awareness.

However, inherent in any crossroad and especially in this cosmic crossroad, is also a point of crisis. The crisis, in my opinion, arises out of the reality that before we can move to the next level of awareness, humankind as a collective consciousness, has to incorporate a "new element" into conscious awareness. Without the integration of this "missing element" into the collective awareness of the psyche of humankind, we cannot and will not make the move that will allow for the journey to the next level of evolution.

Rudolph Steiner, in *Spiritual Hierarchies,* shares this about "the missing element," "***it is humanity's great mission to bring freedom to the world, and, along with freedom, what we call, in the purest sense of the word, LOVE...Freedom and love are two poles that belong together.***"

Twentieth-century metaphysician Charles Fillmore defines *Love*, in its purest sense, in this manner, ***"the Divine in Its feminine aspect [is]...God in Its pure and unconditional aspect of love.***" Thus, the synergy of Steiner and Fillmore's ideas birthed, for me, the idea that the "missing element" in the consciousness of humankind; the element that will allow us to move into the next level of evolutionary awareness – is LOVE – the Feminine nature of the Divine.

The mission of humankind, at this juncture in time, is to awaken to a deeper understanding of the "missing element," ***Love—in its purest sense***, and its role in the cosmic process of evolution. Through free will we have, at our disposal the opportunity to choose to make the decisions that will affect the future of humankind and this planet in the most positive ways – if we choose wisely and begin to birth within the collective psyche, ***Love—in its purest sense.***

There is a catch to all of this, for if this new element of ***Love—in its purest sense***, is to be brought into the psyche of collective awareness, each person, individually, must willing surrender their adverse ego (false ego, the little "me," the self with a small s), and the false beliefs and perceptions that anchors it in place within the personal energy field, to a Higher Source. We must be willing to surrender the adverse ego, in love and through love, to the greater *Wisdom* inherent within each one of us. If we do not evoke this attitude of surrender, then we are choosing to remain caught in the adverse ego's web of duality, with its sense of separation from the Higher Power/God/Higher Dimensional Frequencies.

The adverse ego or, altered ego and the intellect via the adverse ego, keeps us stuck in our head/brain/intellect. "***... the altered ego functions as a seperative, past-tense mechanism of memory ... for all intent and purposes, you may regard the altered-ego [adverse ego] in its entirety as a body of defense mechanisms ... building armor and walls around its territory ... [however] each time a brick is removed, the Golden Light of Wisdom [Love] will pour in ...***"[7]

The seperative nature of the adverse ego keeps us living our lives connected to the lower realm of human emotions and other past-tense memory mechanisms. These lower emotions include fear, hate, despair, depression, greed, mistrust, covetousness, lust, the need for control, and so forth. Thus, the decision to not incorporate ***Love—in its purest sense*** and its elements of compassion, equality, intuition, and integration consciously to our lives, will constitute making the choice at the cosmic crossroad, to take the road of destruction for humankind.

In Valentine Tomberg's work titled *Meditations on the Tarot,* he shared the idea that ***"The exoteric church of Peter*** [the intellect] ***will make way for the 'esoteric' church of John*** [the heart], ***which will be that of perfect freedom."*** This perfect freedom that both Steiner and Tomberg refer to is the freedom to choose to surrender our free will back to the Divine and to consciously choose Love (compassion, equality, intuition) as the force and power at work in our lives.

He goes on to share that this "esoteric church" will not be built on a piece of land, but will be "***built in the interior depths of our heart.***" But we can only build this new church in consciousness as we willingly surrender our heads and hearts to greater service to the One. It is through the heart Chakra/energy mind-center, that we have the ability and potential to touch the pure essence of unconditional love – a.k.a., the feminine nature of the Divine. From contact with the sacred Energy contained within the heart-realm, we receive the gift of intuitive knowing and an unending stream of Grace.

It is time to make new choices. It is time for humankind to consciously choose to surrender to a Greater *Wisdom;* to move the (head) intellect into the realm of the heart (love/wisdom). If, as a species, we are going to survive, it is imperative that humankind consciously begin to join the head with heart.

Symbolically, the head represents intellectual knowledge (masculine traits) and the heart represents intuitive knowing (feminine traits). With the head and the heart working together in a sense of surrender to universal Will, can you envision what levels of awareness humankind will be able to attain and what type of life we will create, for all? All we need to do is to choose to live from a higher state of choice and awareness; and this decision will call forth ***Love—in its purest sense.***

The feminine qualities of the heart (compassion, egalitarianism, intuition, creativity, etc.) ***balanced*** with the masculine qualities (intelligence, power, will, strength, etc.) will allow us to call forth a centered, peace-filled existence within and without. This union will bring about an end to the internal struggle that has existed in our consciousness and that has ultimately revealed itself in the manifestation of our everyday lives and problems. This does not mean we will forever be free of problems, but our method of coping will take on a new form, for we will live from a higher state of awareness.

The union of head and heart has the ability to create an alchemical process of spiritual transformation that will ultimately call forth the living stream of energy of "Gnosis–Cardia," the Greater *Wisdom* of the heart.

It is this Heart–*Wisdom* that will bring ***Love—in its purest sense*** to matter, to human form. This descent of Divine Love, into matter (into our earthen vessels) will form the true "esoteric church." Tomberg said that this esoteric church will be a church of the heart, and it will be built through the sacred union of the head and the heart, the masculine and the feminine joined as One. With the head brought into alignment with the heart, humankind will make the conscious decision to make the turn at the crossroad that will call forth the next phase of being—Love.

The Void of Forgetfulness

Each of us, male and female alike, have a feminine and masculine nature. However, as a society, and as a collective consciousness, we have, over the past several millennia, devalued and pushed aside our feminine nature in favor of the masculine. The feminine qualities of love, unity, and compassion have been all but abandoned by society, while the masculine attributes of will, might, and power are the qualities that we tend to hold in high esteem, honor, and respect.

Masculine attributes and attitudes are very important to the collective whole, but when they become misdirected and misguided, they lead us in the wrong direction. They lead us to a sense of needing to have, own, possess, hold onto, and so forth. These kinds of behaviors, when not balanced with wisdom, engender aggression over peace.

Yet, I do believe that we (collectively and individually) realize on an unconscious level that we are out of balance and that one half of us is lost. We unconsciously realize our mistake on some level, and we are in the process of going in search of balance and our other half, "love, the feminine nature of the divine."

However, instead of searching within for the missing element of divine love, we are still looking to the outer in hopes of finding our fulfillment. We look for "love" in all the wrong places, and we go in search of that ubiquitous something, thinking it "lives" outside of ourselves, in someone or something in this material world. This intense pursuit, leads us to live our lives from what I call the "void of forgetfulness."

The "void of forgetfulness" is a state of consciousness in which we forget and/or feel that we are not complete. When we feel empty, it is like an unquenchable thirst that cannot be met, so in order to feel better about who we are, we fill this "empty place" with things, toys, drugs, booze, money, and this, that, and the other.

In pursuing our need to fill the empty space that engenders the "void of forgetfulness," we have become "***a-holics***"—al-co-holics, rage-a-holics, food-a-holics, sex-a-holics, drug-a-holics, shop-a-holics, and control-a-holics.

Can you see from that list of words that "a-holic" as a suffix tends to connote negative behavior for the word that it is associated with? "A-holic" behavior doesn't fill anything; it is a result of being in the void of forgetfulness.

When we are living in the "void of forgetfulness," we are living the *opposite* of our intended state of Being. We are living *without* knowing the essence of the *Holy* (or whole that is within). We have forgotten this truth, and our *behavior* reflects this forgetting. This forgetting tends to send us out to look in all the wrong places for the answers to our deepest longings, longings that we think will be fulfilled from outside stimuli, but in reality can only be fulfilled from turning within to find our true Beloved, our Self.

When the alcoholics decide that they have taken their "last drink," they make this decision because something within them remembers the truth of their being. A dear friend of mine was, by her own admission, a falling-down drunk alcoholic. One day she went to her dark closet to get a pair of shoes and as she went to pull on the light cord she felt a "bolt of electricity" go through her. She walked out of the closet, changed and ready to claim her sobriety. What happened to her?

I believe that the metaphor of walking into a dark closet and starting to turn on a light was not a coincidence. It represented her willingness to enter into the unknown (the luminous darkness) and find the true light of her being. In the darkness, she embraced her fears and thus remembered the truth of who she was. Because of that remembrance, her life was changed at depth.

She made, in that moment, a conscious choice to begin to take on the characteristics of her "Holiness" rather than her alcoholic-ness or forgetfulness. She released the "a," the attachment to the without, and turned within. She moved from the forgetting, "the a-holic" to "the Holic," one who remembers her (w)holiness.

She remembered that the "void of forgetfulness" could never be filled or satisfied with outside things. She connected with the truth that knows the feeling that stirs the "void of forgetfulness" is, in actuality, a deep longing that lives within our souls to return to Love. And from finding this Love, we are ultimately led to Integrative Spirituality.

And that, my friend, is the answer to the question that Peter Russell asks, "Where are we heading so quickly?" We are heading toward the union of consciousness, the state of living from Integrative Spirituality—where the masculine and feminine aspects of the Divine live together in harmony and balance within each one of us.

The Dark Night of the Soul

"I said to my soul, Be still, and wait without hope,
for hope would be hope for the wrong thing.
And wait without love, for love would be love of the wrong thing.
There is yet faith, but the faith,
and the hope and the love are all found in the waiting.
And do not think, for you are not ready for thought.
So the darkness shall be the light,
and the stillness, the dancing."
—T. S. Elliot

"To change, a person must face the dragon of his appetites."
—Rumi: *A Journal of Poetry* translated by Coleman Barks

Wen self or human consciousness begins the movement towards union or merging with the Higher Self, this stage of development often has associated with it an experience (or for some, experiences) referred to as, a "dying" process; or as St.

John of the Cross so aptly named it, the "Dark Night of the Soul." The dark night of the soul, as many mystics have shared, is unavoidable. The former consciousness is finished and it has to "die." But yet the ego or little self is not willing to be tamed without a fight. It wants to hang on, be in control, and have its last hurrah.

Regardless of how it makes its appearance, ***the Dark Night is a movement in consciousness***—it has nothing to do with (and everything to do with) the emotional upheaval, physical discomfort, or reactions that are elicited no matter what they look like as an experience. The Dark Night, regardless of what the "New Thought Absolutists" say, is a part of the natural progression in the journey to Self and higher levels of awareness.

The Dark Night of the Soul takes as many forms as there are individuals. It may include experiences such as; times of extreme chaos, health challenges, a sense of blind groping or making one's way in the darkness. "Dying" to an old phase of life is never easy—and there is a major difference between a difficult growth experience on the spiritual path and a Dark Night of the Soul.

In a Dark Night experience, it is common for a person to feel a profound sense of disconnection from God, or a feeling that perhaps God doesn't even exist. Yet, even in the midst of feeling the deep sense of separation, there is an awareness that something greater is pulling or pushing one forward in the midst of the pain and confusion of the experience. The Dark Night feels, inwardly, like an obliteration of everything that one once was—and, I guess you could safely say—that is exactly what it is.

The purpose of the Dark Night of the Soul, is to remove the "veils" of false beliefs that we have held firmly in place in consciousness and that have blocked the Light of Truth from shining forth. When the veil is rent, it signifies that the blocks are dissolved and the way is made for Light to shine through the Darkness, however, there is still work to be done. That is why a Dark Night rarely ever happens quickly; it is a process in which we find ourselves involved for weeks, months, and even years. The dark night of the soul comes to us in order that we might grow, know, and put to action the Truth of who we are. It comes for no other reason except that we might grow and learn!

A Madonna Moment

"The price you pay for soul growth
—the pain of birthing and dying—
is worth the gift that is delivered.
But it is always your choice
As to whether or not you will accept the gift."
—T.G.B.

In the midst of a dark night of the soul experience, I began to receive a nudge that I should write about the "burning and tempering" experiences that accompany its appearance. I realize that not everyone goes through the same type of "burnings." However, I thought that perhaps hearing of my first hand experience might help one person–and for me, that would make the effort expended worthwhile.

At first the words were hard to write, for I did not have the strength or the clarity, so I let it go. However, a few weeks later, as the haze began to lift from within my head, the words began to flow, effortlessly and easily. My pen seemed to have a guiding hand as the story unfolded itself through the ink onto the paper. The story describes the depth of my pain and the ensuing emotional roller coaster that evolved from it. It is a descriptive narrative of how it felt as I realized that the "one" in me who was always in control, was now out of control, and I was unable to do anything about it. I would invite you to take a deep breath and allow your heart to read the following words:

An Ode to the Chaos of Change

A haze envelops me, I feel as if a part of me is lost. I cry out in desperation, "Where are you, that familiar part of me that was always in control?" I feel so alone, it feels like a part of me is dying. I know it, I feel it. I wonder, do those around me see it? Do they even notice? To those around me I am a rock, the one that can be counted on. But where did she go, that young one who had the energy to do all things and be all things to everyone. I think to myself that I must find her. I must, I must—or must I?

My "little self" queries, "What kind of a question is that? Of course you must!"

My heart cries out, wondering how long I can live in this state of confusion. I speculate on how long I can survive in this inner state of turmoil. Yet, somewhere from deep within me, something nudges me and says that this state of confusion is not who I really am. But it is who I need to be right now, in this moment.

Afraid, I cry out, "Maybe this is what life will be like from now on."

I am living on an emotional roller coaster. Someone speaks to me, not harshly but firmly, and from somewhere deep within me a feeling is triggered and tears begin to flow. The tears sting and burn my face like a volcano spewing molten lava down a hillside. How could this be? This is not who I am or at least this is not who I have been. You know me—I am the one they describe as a power woman. "Be afraid of her," is often whispered behind my back.

If they could see me now, sitting in my room, wrapped tightly in a blanket, looking like a roly-poly bug curled up for safety under the front door mat. Internally I feel as if I am losing something, but what is it that I am losing? Perhaps it is my sanity. Yet something stirs within me and I feel that, maybe, just maybe, there is something more that is trying to make itself known to me.

The haze that envelops my brain is like a fog rolling in from the sea. I say to myself, "What was I doing? I can't remember! It doesn't matter, it doesn't seem important, yet it does seem that others are counting on me to get things done. So it must be important, I guess. I am so tired, can't you see? You don't see, do you?"

This haze enveloping me feels like an abyss. It is so deep, I wonder, "Will I ever return? This is a scary place to be." In the midst of this turmoil, I cling to the moment and pray for my future. All the while a part of me "knows" that a new way of being is trying to be birthed through me.

My "mind chatter" is relentless; it chants over and over, "Look at you! How can you believe that this is about a Dark Night of the Soul? Get your act back together; you frighten us. You are the rock, the pillar—we can't handle seeing you like this. God forbid what if this would happen to the rest of us in here. You do not need to change; stop this!"

The doctor says, "I have medication that will help your situation, my dear." I hear his words, yet something inside me screams, in response. "Ride me out, embrace me. I am the darkness of the unknown that lives within you. I have come to teach you new things about your self, to teach you about new ways of being inside of your skin and in your heart. Yes, it is true you are enveloped in darkness and it feels very tight. But imagine that you are a caterpillar and that the darkness is your cocoon. Embrace its mystery.

You are in the darkness in order that you might change and transform. It is a natural process to a caterpillar—and to you—if you will but let it be. It is not easy for the new shape of the old caterpillar to escape the cocoon. It takes hard work and days of struggle to emerge from the darkness of the protective wrap. If some passer-by with good intentions tries to help or shorten the process, it only hurts the newly formed butterfly as it works at trying to emerge. A part of you will be lost if you do not embrace where you are and shed the old—alone.

I understand, my child, that you are afraid. I feel the sting of your hot searing tears as they flow down your face. I know they are unwelcome, yet they do bring you a feeling of release and relief. You believe that this person you see in the mirror is not you. The you that you know is strong, in charge and *always* in control.

Dear one, I know that you have never felt like this before—but dying is hard. It requires that you be willing to let go of everything you have held dear about your self and your life. To enter the cocoon demands that you be willing to hang by a string from a limb. I understand that this is very scary. And worst of all, little one, you don't understand why this is happening, do you? But there is something greater within you that does know where you are headed. Can you trust the unknown? The Greatness in you wants all of you, not just a little bit. This same Greatness is encoded in your cellular memory and there is a part of you that knows—it really does!

Fear not these changes—my child—your Beauty lies deep within you and is waiting to be uncovered. When one embraces the darkness and its mystery, she must be willing to feel its feelings, dance with its emotions, and play in its fire. You will see that from surrendering to the process and all it contains, there will come a new light and the dawn of a new day. And as does the butterfly, you too will emerge. Spread your wings and fly."[8]

CHAPTER 2
THE MANY FACES OF THE BLACK MADONNA

The Hidden Mystery of the Black Madonna

"I am black
and
I am beautiful."
—Song of Solomon 1:5: *Hebrew Testament*

"I am black,
I am one with the hidden mystery of the Unknown,
the feminine nature of the Divine
and I am beautiful."
— T. G. B.

"There is no doubt that the prehistoric veneration of
Mother Earth survived intact...
Her power was too ancient and deep
to be altogether destroyed by succeeding patriarchal religions,
including Christianity...
The Black Madonna is this same Earth Mother,
whose blackness represents the color of Earth's fertility."
— Marija Gimbutas: *The Civilization of the Goddess: The World of Old Europe*

The Black Madonna has been venerated in a wide variety of locations and cultures throughout the world and throughout history. At the more than four hundred known shrines dedicated to the Black Madonna, there are several times throughout the year devotees to these sacred sights take pilgrimages. Often the pilgrims, in order to express their devotion to her, traverse the difficult paths to the shrines on foot or on their knees and occasionally they even crawl. All is done to honor her and the gifts that She shares with the world. The pilgrims know that the Black Madonna is the mother of transformation and healing and the power inherent in the energy contained in the luminous darkness. A pilgrimage taken with intention is not only an outer activity but is also an inner journey to the depths of Self.

The pilgrimage to Self does not have a preassigned course. One cannot ask for an itinerary that has had a route charted according to the fastest way or easiest roads. This path cannot be preassigned or even known. The pilgrimage to Self begins with the willingness to surrender to the unknown experience, of the journey. Inherent in this surrender is the idea of trusting each moment and not needing to know what is next. The pilgrim's route is determined by each step that is consciously taken in whatever direction life presents in the moment. The journey requires a deep commitment in order to stay aware of its lessons. It is easy to fall asleep!

Inherent in saying yes to a pilgrimage experience is an internal yearning that is unexplainable. It just *is*. And this unknowingness is understood on every level of your being. Pilgrims know that visiting sacred sites can be a very healing experience for them spiritually, physically, emotionally, and mentally. The Black Madonna's wisdom, energy, and harmony interpenetrate the soil, statuary, buildings, and rocks that surround her sacred space. Her energy can bring to a person a sense of oneness, alignment, and harmony. Pilgrimages to her sacred shrines are known to heal the false perception of a pilgrim's fragmented spirit, soul, and body.

Her shrines are found in large cathedrals, small churches, and monasteries, on mountaintops and in back woods. Geographical locations where She can be found include places such as Chartes Cathedral, Chartes, France; St. Maximin in the Provence region of southern France; Rome, Italy; Avalino, Italy; Amalfi, Italy; the monastery in Einsiedeln, Switzerland; the Black Madonna Shrine in Eureka Springs, Missouri, United States; Montserrat, Spain; the island of Malta; the Cathedral of Mary Magdalene in Vezelay, France; Jasna Gora, Poland; San Juan, Texas, United States; Jalisco, Mexico; Tendari, Sicily; and Istanbul, Turkey.

The Black Madonna's Origins

To paraphrase Shakespeare, ***"a rose by any other name is still a rose."*** There have been throughout history many black goddesses and Black Madonnas. As an archetypal energy, the black goddess/Madonna is an aspect of the feminine nature of the Divine, yet the black goddesses and black Madonnas are unique in the kind of energy they carry. We may refer specifically to the Black Madonna, but her energies can be applied to any of the dark goddesses (e.g., Kali, Tara, Artemis, Isis, Hecate, Pele), and to the ancient Moon mysteries, the Elusion mysteries, and alchemy of the Middle Ages. Her meaning is often discovered through images, myths, dreams, and fantasies. (I honor the Black Madonna specifically because She and Her energies have had a sacred impact on my life. She found me and has not let me go.)

The names that the Black Madonna/Goddesses have been known by and which may have a familiar ring include Our Lady of the Snows, Our Lady of Czestochowa, Our Lady of the Dark Forest, Hagia Sophia, Sophia, Our Lady of Guadalupe, La Divina Pastora, Our Lady Under the Earth, Our Lady of the Pillar, Madonna de San Juan Las Logos, Our Lady of Oropa, Kali, Ishtar, Diana, Isis, Hecate, Green Tara, Artemis, Paravarti, Durga, Sara-Kali, Queen of the Gypsies, the Veiled Goddess, the Black Virgin, the Wailing Widow, the Dark Woman of Knowledge, Sophia Nigrans, Black Sophia, the Crone, Notre Dame de Montserrat,

Black Madonna of Chartes, the Outcast Daughter, Sophia Stellarium, Sophia of the Stars, the Black Goddess—just to name a few.

Each of the above-mentioned are examples of different names and types of Black Madonnas; historically, they were venerated by and come from the Christian tradition, pagan cults, the troubadours of Provence, the Knights Templar (warrior–monks), ancient goddess worship, Buddhism, Hinduism, Egyptology, the Cathars, and others. Yet, as much as they differ culturally, they all have one common denominator. They carry the archetypal energies of the dark goddess, which is empowerment through transformation and healing, life and birth, death and rebirth. She is also a holder of energy that allows one to come to peace with his or her issues regarding sexuality and sensuality.

In the time of the Ancient Mother, when the feminine nature of the Divine aspect of humankind was revered, her dark color was associated with the color black which represented fertility and growth. Caves, triangles, horns, the Moon, and the chevron were symbols that reflected this aspect of her fertility and darkness. The people of these ancient times knew that the darkness and its associated symbols would bring to them a sense of balance, wisdom, abundance, and wholeness.

The Black Madonna's true origin is virtually unknown, although there are many opinions surrounding the details of her beginnings. One school of thought states that She descends from the worship of Isis in Egypt. Ancient wooden statues of her have been found in Sparta, Greece, and are believed to be the goddess Artemis, her early protégée. Esoteric groups such as the Druids worshiped The Black Mother and called her Our Lady Under The Earth. Others believe that her route started in Mesopotamia, and then moved across the Mediterranean Sea gracing the isles and lands of Greece, Sicily, Malta, and Italy. She made her way to Spain and France and then shared her energy with Central Europe and Russia.

Another opinion has it that She was brought from the Holy Land during the Crusades in the eleventh century. At that time, She became very popular as the Black Virgin. She was thought to be a dark-skinned goddess who "bridged spirituality and sexuality." The gifts She bestowed included the blessing of fertility in pregnancy, in crops, and in the "delight in the mysteries of the body." She was perceived as independent and one who stood alone in her strength. Certainly She was the other side of the virginal, chaste and obedient Madonna coin. In truth it appears that the more the Papal dictates of the Catholic Church proclaimed the veneration of the Virgin Mary as the idealized woman, the more prominent the Black Madonna became as an underground symbol. Shrines to the Black Madonna and Virgin proliferated, as hundreds were built throughout Europe in the twelfth and thirteenth centuries, and a few still stand today.

However, many of her icons were destroyed during the time of the Inquisition, for Her popularity was a threat to the church fathers. They felt that She was a threat to the male-only authority of the priesthood.

"In Catholic countries, where blackness...
is associated almost exclusively with magic and the occult,
Black Madonnas are considered especially wonder-working,
as the possessors of hermetic knowledge and power."
—Marina Warner: *Alone of All Her Sex: The Myth and Cult of the Virgin Mary*

A Madonna Moment

In *The Black Madonna,* Fred Gustafson shares the story of an interview with an astronaut who just returned from outer space and was asked, "***Have you seen God?***" and the astronaut responded, "***Yes, and She is black.***"

I know that feeling; it came as an overwhelming awareness to me when I was doing research on a Black Madonna known as Pele. When I say research, it was not so much an intellectual pursuit as it was an internal desire to know of her and her gifts.

Pele is the "goddess of Earthquakes"; when your life is stale, you can call on her energies to help shake things up. Pele knows that after the appearance of eruption and disorder, that nature will always seek to find a new balance. Hot molten lava, interruptions of status quo flow heavily during her periods of activity; however, She will always bring things back, albeit from a new level of awareness.

Shortly after I began to invoke the archetypal energies of Pele, I went to the IMAX theatre to see *The Fires of Kuwait.* It was a documentary on the fires that occurred in the oil fields in Kuwait; as they were depicted, they were devastating. The film was so well done, you could almost feel the intense heat of the fire as the sounds of the flames roared in the background. The massiveness of the field of destruction was overwhelming. Watching the firefighters struggle against something bigger than they was awesome. Charred, black soot oozed from every corner and all vegetation was lost. Miles and miles of devastation made it seem as though everything was gone, with no hope of survival of any life.

Have you ever experienced a time in your life that felt like the scene that I have just described? Perhaps Pele was trying to make her self known, or perhaps She is working to make herself known to you, right now. Know that regardless of the appearance, there is a happy ending to your story, for Pele always brings balance. And so it was with the fires in Kuwait. The last segment of the movie pans the fields of devastation, and then the camera moves in and focuses on a burnt log. There in the midst of the charred remains that looks like ultimate devastation without a sense of hope is a little green sprout lifting its head, calling forth new life, revealing strength and new optimism.

Sophia and the Black Madonna: Two Sides of One Coin

"The image of the Black Virgin embodies the ageless Wisdom of life,
the ageless Wisdom of an invisible dimension hidden within the outward form of nature,
which brings it to being, informs and guides it, or contains it, as a mother her child....
At the same time the Black Virgin symbolizes the fathomless mystery of the soul,
which must follow the star that guided the wise men
if it is to understand these mysteries and itself give birth to the Divine child."
—Anne Baring and Jules Cashford: *The Myth of the Goddess: Evolution of an Image*

These words that follow come from the Nag Hammadi Library texts found in 1945 in Egypt. Written two thousand years ago, the words reflect Sophia's thoughts about Herself.

"For I am the first and the last.
I am the honored one and the scorned one.
I am the whore and the holy one.
I am the wife and the virgin.
I am the barren one and many are her sons....
I am silence that is incomprehensible.
I am the utterance of my name."
—Nag Hammadi Library

"The Lord created Earth by Wisdom...
The Lord made me first of all."
—Proverbs 3:19 and Proverbs 8:22: *Hebrew Testament*

Sophia is Greek for *Wisdom*, She is said to represent *Wisdom* that has never turned its face from the Law. *Wisdom* gets Her inspiration for creation, and Her ability to unfold creation, by keeping Her gaze ever fixed on the immutable Law. It has been said that to discover *Wisdom* is to discover *Self.*

One of the most enlightening definitions of *Wisdom* that I have come across in my years of study comes from Hilary Hart. She defines *Wisdom* as, ***"understanding the emptiness of reality—with the skillful means side—the ability to bring that wisdom to the world, to your everyday life."***[9]

King Solomon desired *Wisdom* above all else. When he was given the opportunity to choose anything in the world, he chose *Wisdom*—he chose an understanding heart. He desired to know at his deepest level, the emptiness of reality, that the world holds nothing of great importance. It is out of this wisdom around "emptiness" that true compassion arises.

This is not the type of compassion that is attached to an emotion that desires a certain outcome, but this is compassion without attachment—a compassion that arises because the beholder knows the truth of what "emptiness of reality" really means; thus the one in whom this compassion is aroused is able to love the sinner as well as the holy one equally.

Acting from the state of compassionate wisdom, we are detached from worldly desires and judgments. Thus detachment is free to flow forth and is able to take action in the world. ***"Compassionate action. You are not acting for yourself, but for others."***[10]

When we are awakened to the wisdom of the "emptiness of reality," we are able to glean the true relationship in the appearance of opposite energies. We are able to retranslate the appearance of the opposites and see that in truth these opposites are actually complements. We are aware that the energy of seemingly opposing natures (masculine–feminine, immanent–transcendent, light–darkness), in fact, works in tandem to co-create the universe.

Most people from Western society have very little knowledge of the Divine in Its feminine aspect. Whereas, Eastern religions have long known of the balance of the universe and the sacredness contained within the union of the Divine Masculine and the Divine Feminine. Because of this understanding, they have the feminine aspect of the Creator as a core aspect of their belief systems. For example, Hinduism has Shiva and Shakti; the Tao speaks of the Tao and Teh as the One that creates the Supreme Mystery.

One of the first mentions in history of Sophia occured around 600 B.C.E. In *Trinisophia*, Robert Powell shares that the word *philosophy* had its origin in Greece. Pythagoras, the Father of Mathematics, coined the term that means the "love of Sophia" or the love of *Wisdom*. Pythagoras knew that if one opened his or her heart to the Divine Mother, one would have access to all wisdom.

For several millennia prior to the birth of Jesus, society had chosen to put aside the feminine aspect of the Godhead and had begun to call forth only the masculine aspect. Occasionally, the feminine nature of the Divine would rear Her head, however, She would be quickly silenced or debunked in some manner or fashion. We as a collective modern society bought this story of a Divine-Masculine (***only***) Deity—hook, line, and sinker. Living in this half-truth, we silenced the feminine nature of the Divine and with her a part of our selves.

"It is that putting away of Sophia (Wisdom)
that has created the unbalance in us.
As we move toward the new millennium,
the cry to return to balance is being uttered.
The Divine Feminine, Sophia, is rearing her head
and asking—no, demanding!—to be recognized"
—Catlin Matthews: *Sophia, Goddess of Wisdom*

Humankind as a collective consciousness has "fallen." We have removed our attention from the Truth of our being (Law/Principle) and lost our connection with the stream of "Living Fire," the life force that is the essence of our eternal nature. Lost in the realm of matter, we have turned our attention from that which is Real and have become mired in that which appears to be real.

King Solomon knew that Sophia/*Wisdom* was the greatest gift that one could receive. When given the chance to have anything in the world bestowed on him, he requested to know *Wisdom*. Rather than having dominion over all the riches in the world of materiality, King Solomon chose to have an understanding heart—he chose to know Sophia/*Wisdom*. King Solomon knew that knowing Sophia/*Wisdom* as a living Presence would awaken a stream of living Energy within him that was a mixture of the fire, the breath, and the power of the Holy Spirit and this Energy would reveal to him the Glory of God.

In the fourth century B.C.E., Sophia was introduced to the Judaic culture and religion. She was revered as a hypostate of God, a personification of God. Sophia and her mighty works are found in the Hebrew Testament in Proverbs (fourth century B.C.E.); Ben Sirach, or Ecclesiastics (second century B.C.E.); and the *Wisdom* of Solomon (first century B.C.E.); just to name a few. From the moment of her introduction, Sophia grew in stature and importance. By the first century, B.C.E., Sophia stood as a rival to the reigning Greek and Egyptian goddesses of the time.

This feminine aspect of God–*Wisdom* was also referred to in the Hebrew Testament by other names such as El Shaddai, Yahweh (a balance of both the masculine and feminine), Ruah, and Hokhmah. However, over the centuries these words with their feminine connotation of God have lost their original meaning and context. For instance, El Shaddai has been interpreted as the Almighty, God of the Mountain. However, *Shad* in Hebrew means "breast," and *ai* is an ancient Hebrew feminine word, ending. Therefore, El Shaddai, rightly interpreted, would mean "the breasted one." Yahweh had a connotation of a Divine Being with a maternal or womb-like quality. Although not any longer spoken of in this way, both hold feminine contexts.

The Hebrew word for the Holy Spirit, Ruah, is feminine in nature and means "the essence through which the Divine acts." Ruah is mentioned 378 times in the Hebrew Testament. This feminine Spirit of God eventually became known as *Wisdom* and is also referred to in the Hebrew Testament by the word *Hokhmah*. If one takes all the word references made to an aspect of *Wisdom* or the feminine nature of the Divine found in the Hebrew Testament, She is mentioned more times than Abraham, Moses, Isaac, Jacob, Noah, or David. Yet, I ask you, as a child were you taught about the importance or the significance of Sophia or the feminine face of God? I would venture to say that your answer is no!

What happened to Sophia? How did we lose this feminine aspect of the Divine when She obviously was so important? Sophia's fall from grace is thought to have begun when Philo, a philosopher living in the first century, C.E., started writing his philosophic dissertations. These writings clearly began to shift the power base from Sophia because he assigned Her attributes to Jesus Christ. It was from Philo's writings that other early Christian organizers were influenced and championed his words, thoughts, and beliefs.

Philo's writing contained incredibly inflammatory remarks about the female gender and its role in society. Here is an excerpt citing Philo's *Fuga on Wisdom.* It is from a book by Joan Chamber Engelsman, *The Feminine Dimension of the Divine:*

"While Wisdom's name is feminine, her nature is manly. For that which comes after God, occupies a second place and therefore was termed feminine to express contrast with the maker...who is masculine. For preeminence always pertains to the masculine and the feminine always comes short of and is lesser than it." *Writings of Philo, Fuga 50–52*

The transfer of power was solidified by the early theologians of the third century who defined the beliefs and the major precepts of Christianity. Although there were many different sects and thoughts about Jesus and his mission, two major trains of thought prevailed during the early years of Christianity.

The first train of thought came from a group known as the Gnostics. The Gnostics believed that Jesus was a Way-shower. His mission was to bring to the people the message that contained the idea that *Wisdom* was hidden within—and could be known by all people—regardless of sex or race, Gnosticism leadership was open to all, men and women alike.

The second group, known as the Orthodox group, held the belief that Jesus suffered and died for our sins. In this theology, humankind needed an intermediary and was seen as a sinner. This was the belief that eventually became the dogma of traditional religion.

The beliefs of this second group became prominent when they were selected as the only true religious teachings by Emperor Constantine in 325 C. E. Because of Constantine's influence and ability to move this newly forming religious movement worldwide, these Orthodox beliefs eventually became the dogma and underpinning of what is known today as Christianity theology.

Over the years and centuries the influence of Philo's writings succeeded in removing Sophia from her sacred perch and changed the course of Judaic

Christianity. This newly created Divine Son aspect of God usurped the power and stature of the feminine nature of the Divine and She was all but eliminated from our minds and hearts. *Wisdom* and the feminine nature of the Divine were silenced!

Wisdom speaks her words to us in a variety of forms. Often, She whispers softly, yet speaks with a firm authority. Sometimes we hear her words screaming in the depths of our being. Or sometimes She speaks without uttering a word, and we feel Her nonverbal vibrations coming from the deepest part of who we are. Many have desired her, have sought her and not found her, for *Wisdom* comes when She is ready, not when She is commanded. Sophia was and is the desire of the heart to express its true wisdom. She is the motivator of creation and the movement of it also.

Sophia, in Her wisdom, is intuition, pure love, deep knowledge, plus She holds the gifts of awakening, arousing, destroying, and transforming in her bosom. We fear these gifts, because at our deepest levels we do not want to change and we know that contact with Sophia will cause a movement in consciousness.

As archetypal energy, the feminine nature of the Divine is a continuum with both the glory of the Virgin as pure Love and the Black Madonna as the primal energy of life experience desiring to teach us of Love. As one assuming two roles, She rises above dualism, for She is like one coin with two sides: the both/and—not the either/or. Therefore, the feminine nature of the Divine is the heart of the creative process, the wisdom and way-show-er of the inner quest, and the birther and destroyer of creation.

Wisdom and the Black Madonna live in the mystery, the unknown and are also the earthly aspect of the goddess in the material world. In her earthly aspect, *Wisdom* may appear as sensual and seductive, putting forth her siren's call.

Sophia is our deep wisdom, the deep longing within each of us that creates the yearning—the yearning that gets so misinterpreted, for it is the yearning to come home to Self. She is mystical living spirit, which permeates each of us. She guides us as pilgrims on the journey of awakening, yet She remains unknown to us until we awaken to Her Presence within our hearts. In the midst of the appearance of darkness and unknowingness (the tools of transformation and change used by the Black Madonna), Sophia is willing to share her wisdom and insights and to lend guidance, if the pilgrim will but listen.

Sophia's words promise us that She will lead us to what we need. "I will give thee the treasures of the darkness...and hidden riches of the secret places." What is this secret place that She speaks of? It is that place that resides deep within our hearts where we discover and uncover the truth of our being.

This secret place is referred to as the darkness, for it is buried in the unfathomable depths of our heart-space, it is a mystical point not contained within the confines of time and place, yet it can be found by turning within. It is the center point where we ***know*** that we are one with God. This secret place is metaphorically described as a seed that has been planted within our being and that is waiting for the perfect moment to open, break forth, and bring new life.

Sophia knows Her powers and how to use them. She begins by trying to seduce us not in a sensual way, but as the seductive pull of the One Desire. This Desire is the one that is spoken of in the *Tao Te Ching*. It is Desire that calls us to new ways of being and to new levels of awareness; however, the true nature of this Desire of the Tao has been forgotten.

The result of this "fall" from remembrance has spiraled humankind to the depths of a consciousness of materiality. With the real message of Desire being lost, all of creation suffers, for through the misinterpretation of desire on the physical plane and what it is that we are longing for, we are continually crucified through the processes of our life experiences. These outer crucifixions will continue until we as a collective consciousness choose to resurrect our thinking and return to the path of *Wisdom*.

Sophia knows full well what returning to Her way of wisdom requires. She knows that the pilgrims on the path of Return may need to be broken open or broken down (egoistically) in order for a new awareness in consciousness to be birthed. *Wisdom* inherently knows that one cannot put "new wine in old wine skins" and that this requires change.

Thus, Her seductive pull may take the form of being drawn to a new job—where once you get there, instead of it being in paradise, everything falls apart. Her siren's call may come in the form of an illness, where the pilgrim is stripped of all that he thought was important in life. The pilgrim is ill and unable to move for lack of energy, taken to a place of forced stillness, internal and external quietness, where one learns of the gift of humility. In these moments of perceived helplessness, often the pilgrim is not left with any other choice except to reach out to others and ask for their help. Humility is only one of many gifts that can come when one cannot do for one's self for a period of time, and Sophia is fully aware of this!

Sophia has, within her wisdom, an understanding that allows Her to walk with the pilgrim through dark nights of the soul, the times of unknowingness, the places of darkness, and in the trials of the mystery. In these moments, She pushes, urges, and helps to create the longing and desire to have our spiritual potential fulfilled.

The problem is that we tend to misinterpret the cues of the call, looking outside ourselves when we feel these longings, perceiving that something or someone in the outer world can fill the desires we are feeling. So we fill our lives with drugs, alcohol, work, love affairs, shopping, anything and everything that can help to anaesthetize ourselves from the Self, hoping, in some way, to fill or heal the gaping hole we feel inside. This hole seems to grow bigger each day that we ignore its existence. We have not remembered or been taught that what we desire is within us, not outside.

When we realize that there is something that doesn't quite fit anymore and are willing to initiate the quest to find out what it is, we can be assured that the feminine nature of the Divine and one of her healers is with us. In this moment of realization, we can *know* that the feminine nature of the Divine is embracing us and coming to us in one of her various forms. She is using Her positive powers of seduction, her siren's call, to entice us to go deeper within ourselves to contact and find our true wisdom.

The Dance of *Wisdom*

When we say yes to participating in the dance of *Wisdom*, we find that it is a rhythmic swaying which moves us between two poles—that of being filled and then being emptied—and then filled again in order that we might still be emptied. While being emptied, chances are that we will be brought to a state of our lowest common denominator (we may experience some sort of turmoil, pain, or suffering). Ken Wilbur, contemporary writer and mystic, says that spiritual evolution and growth, "is very messy." To believe that we will live in a state of Nirvana or bliss, without pain or heartache, is to deny an important aspect of our spiritual growth – the part being human plays in the spiritualization of matter.

In this state of emptiness, we find that we are stripped of all illusions that we might have about what is important in life in the moment, or we may be taken to a place of inability to do life, as we have previously known it. Here in this space of vulnerability, *Wisdom* teaches us in ways that are unique to Her. Stories of Her confrontations include being depleted of resources or energy, reduced to bare minimums, or being forced to non-productivity. We think, "How awful!"

Yet is it? For in bringing us to our knees, She is asking us to look at how we have been living life. She asks us to look at the questions like, "Who am I?" and "What is important in this moment?" In fact, they become a mantra, as over and over these questions resound within as we reconstruct the fragments of our shredding false beliefs until finally we are ready to surrender to the lesson and to the practice of nonresistance.

What we find is that in these moments of surrender clarity comes. Insights and "Aha's," Her gifts, are made available to us. She makes insights like the following available for us: "I have learned to rest, and to be willing to do God's Will." "I know that I do not need to control or manipulate life any longer." "Life will not end if I do not say yes to everything that people want me to do." "I have learned to set boundaries and how to say no."

Wisdom also holds replenishment and growth in her bosom. She is our time of being filled, of renewal, of knowing that we are being moved to new levels of awareness and loving it. Hers seems to be the positive way. But is it? Many times we do not learn the depths of a lesson until something is taken from us or we are forced to review or take inventory of our lives.

The Initiation

Have you ever experienced one of those special "initiations" or tests of life? Maybe you are in the midst of one right now? Know that inherent in its coming is a gift that can result in changing you at depth, if you are open to receiving it!

In sharing the following story from my life, please remember that these words are shared from a sense of deep humility. In addition, I know that any words that I might use to describe what happened to me are awkward and empty. They cannot in any way convey the essence of the sacredness of the experience. In fact, in the context of what happened, they are very inadequate as a vehicle of expression.

On Dec. 7th, 2001, I had what was to be minor surgery. The morning after the surgery I was in pain and yet feeling very peaceful, very at One with God. My husband came in to the hospital room and said he thought that I did not look well. To him I appeared to be very swollen and congested. He was so concerned that he went out to find the nurse. She came in took my vital signs and with a finger monitor, she measured my blood oxygen content. The blood oxygen content was 84%, dangerously low. Immediately she placed an O^2 canula under my nose and rushed me off to x-ray. From there I was moved me to CCU, the Cardiac Intensive Care Unit. The diagnosis, they shared with us was Congestive Heart Failure.

I wanted to be afraid, but I couldn't, I didn't know why, I only knew that there was a strange feeling of peace that accompanied me all the rest of the day. Sometime in the middle of night, I remember waking and being aware of how dark it was in the room. It felt as if I were in a cocoon. Lying there in the darkness, I felt guided to look at the words, Congestive – Heart – Failure, from a metaphysical perspective.

I took each word and asked what, if any, meaning did the word hold or have for me and/or my life. e.g., Congestive — What congestive thoughts, words, or deeds had I been holding in my heart? How had these thoughts congested me? As I was moving through the exercise, a Voice began to speak to me. It resounded throughout my being. It was the Still Small Voice of my Higher Power and it was definitely a Feminine Voice.

The Voice said, "Look higher, go deeper and trust Me. Let Mystery be your Guide." In a flash I knew what the Voice meant. To continue to look at effect, by asking about the meaning of everything at the level of the problem, was not the highest way. To look at the nuances of the problem, kept me looking at the level of appearance and true healing, soul healing, does not reside there.

I felt Her Energy invite me to move from the desire to ask questions about the level of effect – the dis-ease – and to turn my attention to the level of Cause; to the level of God. I was being asked to turn to the mystical level of prayer. The mystical level of prayer, "takes no thought" about anything, it is a state of total surrender. In surrender, one does not pray for health, or healing, or anything else; one only prays to know God; to experience the conscious realization of God.

In an instant, I was moved into a meditative/altered state. The words, "'I' in the midst of me," began to arise from the depths of my being. Consciously and with intention I placed my attention on my heart space, I moved the word "I" from my head into the vastness of my heart space.

Immediately I felt the mighty "I" begin to vibrate within every cell of my being. The "I," in the midst of my heart began to grow and expand, until it consumed all of me. Once the "I" consumed me, there was not – "I" and toni. – there was only "I." Toni, as I knew her, disappeared and what was left was no-thing and everything. All boundaries, limitations, and desires dissolved and all that was left was the Great Vibration of the One "I," emitting a profound frequency of Peace.

In a flash, a deep understanding of the words, "I am the Way," filled my being. "I" ***is*** the way. "I" is the secret to the spiritual message given to us by Jesus Christ. "I" came to set us free. "I" came to break the shackles of misunderstanding and limitation and when rightly understood, everything vibrates at a higher level.

Toni was no longer under the dominion of circumstances or disease; she was now in the vibration of Grace. Grace, a palpable vibration moved through out "my" energy field, blessing everything in Its path. Toni – as the world knew her – disappeared into a state of ecstasy.

In this space of heightened awareness, there was full knowing. ALL POWER IS IN GOD – were not just words – it was a "living" energy field. In this field of vibration, there was *NOT* GOD and something else to overcome, there was ONLY GOD! I – toni had disappeared, now there was only "I." The "I" that knows – the Father and "I" are One. The "I" that knows – there is no duality, there is only ONE!

"I" is eternal life, so what is there to get? Nothing, we have it all! I knew that there was not God ***and*** ... there is only God; God, the One Presence and One Power.

Toni was One with everything and she was no-thing. Jesus Christ said, "I of myself can do nothing." And "He who sees me, sees the Father." In this Holy moment, I totally knew what Jesus meant. I saw It, I felt It, I knew It. I was bathed in It, caressed by It, embraced by It and I was It. It – Peace. It, the fullness of Divine Love.

If there is only God, and God Is, then what do I need? The fullness of God is present here and now. How could there be a healing to get, when God *IS* Life and "I," in the midst my being and your being, is that same Life?

No, there was nothing to get, for there is no difference between life and death. They are both unfolding states of awareness. I knew that to desire one more than the other was to be attached (thru belief) to the illusions of this world. No there is no thing to desire. Nothing! I knew in the moment that the "I" which "I" am is all and all that I ever need.

Just as Jesus threw the moneychangers out of the temple, so toni too, must clear the temple of the idea of "a merchandise-mart concept of prayer and of God." Immediately I knew I could no longer pray for my health or my life, for what did I know of the workings of God. It took this mysterious ailment to bring to me this experience of God. How would I know that death might not do the same or more?

How could I ever ask for anything again? How could I know what was best for my life or anyone else's? Life is Eternal and because of that there is nothing to fear — ever. In that moment, my vibrational energy field was changed forever. I knew that there was, is, and ever will be, only one desire for my life – to know more of the Divine – and to revel in Its fruits. The fruits of Spiritual Light, Spiritual *Wisdom*, Spiritual Intuition, Spiritual Discernment and so much more.

I realized God never healed anyone. What kind of God would heal some people and not others? NO! Disease is not a power to overcome, for there is only One Power and that Power is Divine Love, which emanates as Divine Life.

God-Power doesn't overcome anything; not poverty, sickness, or discord. Each person must realize, in consciousness, that "appearance" is not a power to overcome. It is something to be understood and when we understand it, it disappears. There is not God and error; there is only Universal Energy awaiting our receptivity in consciousness. That explained to me why some are healed and others aren't.

Jesus never said, "God will heal you." He said, "Stretch forth your hand." "Your faith has made you whole." Your faith! Therefore, I am personally responsible for my life. Nor did he say, "God will forgive you." He said, "Neither do I condemn you, go and sin no more." And "You shall know the truth and the truth will set you free."

How did the story end? While in the hospital, I went through a myriad of heart tests and x-rays, a nuclear stress test, echocardiogram, pulmonary this's and that's – and they could find anything wrong with my heart. Nothing — NO-Thing! No earthly explanation for why it happened. But I knew! The experience was part of the Divine plan — it was a teacher that had come to share a life-lesson.

Over the years, The Energy of the Feminine nature of the Divine has bestowed many gifts upon me, and each gift ultimately taught me how to live from the wisdom of my heart. At times, the Energy has taken me by the hand and at other times by the throat, forcing me to move with the rhythmic flow of the universal energies. Then It would ask me to stand perfectly still in the midst of chaos and trust Its power. These were new concepts for me.

I know now, in the deepest core of my Being, that prayer is an energy, a vibration that, when set in motion through a combination of factors, calls forth healing. Something has shifted inside of me. A deeper, wisdom-laden energy, an aspect of my being that knows the truth about Divine Life has been called forth, and it causes me to remember the Truth of who I AM.

Prayer is both spiritual and scientific. Prayer as a treatment combines "right elements" and has the power to shift the energetic-frequencies within the body on both a subtle and cellular level. Whether we believe it not, we all live our lives attached to the appearance of that which is before us. Prayer has the power to change our mundane expectations and attachments and shift them to higher states of consciousness. From this higher state of awareness, perspectives change. Certainly my mundane perspectives of reality changed.

I now see more beauty in life. I hear the music in the wind, the symphony in a rainstorm. I see the glory in the blossoms of the morning flowers covered with dew. I feel the radiance of love moving within my cellular structure and that movement brings me to tears over the simplest of things. Me, the nurse who responded to code blues without an ounce of fear and who worked the emergency room without flinching at the sight of blood and gore. I am now moved to tears at a baby's smile and feel a cringe in my heart when someone describes their pain. Oh, yes, I have been healed—physically, mentally, emotionally, and spiritually.

Divine Love, as energy, is impersonal and not sentimental. It worked and continues working for my body and it will work for you. The energy of your prayer can connect with the impersonal energy of Divine Love and your sacred intent will carry it forward. Through this combination, you will be lifted into a higher vibrational frequency, (in accordance with your soul choices) where wholeness and perfection is the natural state of your Being.

Since 1995, She, the Divine Mother of Matter, has been burning me in Her fires, teaching me tough lessons; and they have been coming through my body, in the form of health challenges. Some people learn their lessons through prosperity challenges, relationships and betrayal, and other sundry forms of "devastation." Mine has been through my body.

Each time a dark night comes, each time a "burning" occurs and I willingly surrender and walk through it; I learn a deeper soul lesson. Another layer of subconscious shadow muck gets peeled away. Are there ever moments when I wish that the "burnings," would stop or go away? Sometimes, when I forget and fall into feeling sorry for myself! However, those moments are few and far between now. For then I remember the Truth of what they come for – that the Glory of God might be revealed through this instrument.

Then, I think, "What if stopping the lessons would mean that I would have no further soul growth? That I would not experience those moments of union and ecstasy with the Beloved;" and then something in me cries out. "Then, never, I say, never. Burn me Beloved, in the fires of transformation that I might realize and make real, more of who You are. Let only your sacred Energy flow through this vessel. Erase me and let only Thee shine forth."

I live in a constant state of remembering and forgetting, of reuniting and tearing apart. Life is change and change is unpredictable and so I continue to breathe. What does the Divine want from me? To do exactly this—breathe, just learn to stay centered, taking one breath after another. In the midst of all the trials and tribulations of life, keep breathing.

What I have learned is that somehow, in the midst of that space of breathing, I am changed, transformed, and renewed. The wisdom of having experienced transformation and learning the lesson inherent in it is the gift that the Divine has bestowed upon me.

Mary, Mother of Christ, the Cosmic Mary and the Black Madonna

"Perhaps the most powerful and all-embracing of all symbols of the Virgin that is 'returning' to our Christian consciousness to help us re-imagine the power of the Divine feminine is that of the Black Madonna."

—Andrew Harvey: *Son of Man, the Mystical Path to Christ*

Andrew Harvey and his teachings on the re-emergence of the Sacred Feminine in Christianity have touched me profoundly and influenced me greatly. What I have found in their midst has given me a new sense and perspective regarding the historical Mary, the Cosmic Mother/feminine nature of the Divine, and their relationship to the Black Madonna. Harvey's book, *Son of Man: The Mystical Path to Christ* came to me as I was writing this manuscript and I know now that it was not by accident that it came to my hands—and from Harvey himself.

According to Harvey, the Black Madonna/Black Virgin is the most powerful and sublime aspect of the Cosmic Mary, a.k.a., the Divine Mother/feminine nature of the Divine. As an iconic image, the Black Madonna is the dark-skinned Virgin sitting on a throne, arrayed in regal splendor with a child in her lap. The first images of her in this state of royal stature and splendor are believed to have come from the painters of the sixth, seventh, and eighth centuries C.E. Why She began to be represented in this fashion seems to be unknown.

The Black Madonna in this image stands for both a mother arrayed in all her magnificence and a mother who has diligently guarded, sustained, and nourished the rhythms of nature. Over the centuries, women who have understood their roles of guardians of the rhythms of nature have gone to her to ask that She bless them with fertility, that they are able to bear a child.

The Black Madonna is represented as the dark-skinned Virgin, with a sense of power and mystery that comes from an unknown source. It is this aspect of the dark-skinned Virgin (as the mysterious, the unknown, the void, and the womb-like darkness) that is found in the many cathedrals dedicated to her all over Europe. The cathedrals of Europe built in the twelfth and thirteenth centuries have had this image of the Black Madonna as a form of Mary worship at the core of their spiritual practices since their inception.

During her earlier times, one of the secret meanings that the Black Madonna held was that of representing for women, the freedom to express their sensuality and sexuality. She was the bride, the maternal mother. She did not represent the idealized woman of the "Virgin Mother." The "Virgin Mother" notion had been being acknowledged in the church, but did not come to "mainstream" thinking until the fourteenth century C.E. when Mary was elevated to that position by the church Fathers, through the adoption of the Immaculate Conception doctrine.

A backlash to this elevated Virgin Mary, Queen of Heaven, chaste Mother theory was that the shadow side of this ideology emerged and brought with it the Virgin's opposite—the Witch. The mystery and darkness of the feminine known as the Black Madonna was lost, the touchable became the untouchable. And to prove how revered the "Virgin Mother" was, her dark shadow side, the Witch, was hunted down, hanged, or burned at the stake—lest anyone forget what price must be paid for obedience to God and to the Church.

Over time, the Black Madonna as a feminine symbol and icon has been misunderstood, misinterpreted, ignored, and her true meaning repressed. It is only now that mystics and followers of the spiritual path are turning to her, for She is appearing to them, in her dark-skinned beauty, in dreams, visions, and symbols. Her new-found seekers are attempting to internally integrate and assimilate everything that is being discovered about her.

One of the deeper meanings of the return of the Black Madonna in consciousness today is that men and women alike are going to Her—not as many have done in the past to ask for help in child birth or conception—but in order that their consciousness may be prepared to become the fertile ground that gives birth to the Cosmic Christ.

Jesus was the first fruit of the womb of the historical Mary. It was Mary (representing our feminine nature) that was prepared to gestate and then to deliver to the world the message of the Good News, the Christ consciousness and Its glorious splendor. It is said that if one wants to eat of a certain fruit, one must first find the tree. Mary (our feminine nature) is the tree (the spiritual growing place within us) and to find her enables us to eat of the fruit, her first-born, the Christ (the matured spiritual qualities that ripen in consciousness and that are the "living flame" imbued within the heart).

Regarding the make-up of the Holy Trinity, I have facetiously stated over the years that if there is a Father and Son there has to be a Mother hiding in there somewhere. The world is a microcosm of the macrocosm, and it takes both a mother and father to create a child. By leaving the Divine or Cosmic Mother out of the Holy Trinity and Christian teachings, I have always felt that we have lost a significant portion and an important depth in the understanding of who we are as spiritual beings. The historical Mary was and is the epitome of the Sacred Feminine and is the Cosmic Mary that now desires to return in full bloom to the hearts and minds of humankind.

The Cosmic Mystical Mother Mary and the historical Mary embody within their teachings the traits and aspects of the Black Madonna. When one begins to understand the real meaning of the historical Mary and the Cosmic Mary contained in the image of the Black Madonna and its *full* significance, what one sees is that in the image of the Black Madonna are all of the different aspects of the Divine Motherhood. Then and only then does one begin to understand the Black Madonna and her true mission, fire, and glory.

In his tape *The Radiant Heart,* Harvey refers to the idea that there are "fundamentally different but totally linked ways" in which you can see the *fullness* of the Black Madonna characterized in the qualities of the feminine nature of the Divine, the Cosmic Mother (appearing with the face of Mary), and the historical Mary. All three images of the universal Marys, when they are coalesced and united, blaze forth with a new and deeper mystical meaning of the Black Madonna. These characterizations include the following.

She Is the Queen of Darkness and Mystery:

The Black Madonna, as is the Cosmic Mother, is known as the darkness, the void, the birther of the cosmos, the final mystery of the Divine Love of God, the transcendent Kali–Mother, and the womb out of which all creation is made and formed. She stands as and for the ordeal of the sacred darkness that we enter again and again and again, each time going deeper and deeper to the mystery of the spiritual path. As the Queen of transcendent "dark" awareness that lives in the unconscious, She is the ultimate knowledge, the ultimate mystery, and the ultimate mystical passion of life expressing itself.

She Is the Queen of Tantra and of Nature:

The Black Madonna, as is the Divine Feminine, is known as and for the darkness of the fields that bear the fruitful harvest, the richness of the menstrual blood, the dark mystery of all the natural processes inherent in her and in life. She is the blesser of transformations in external and inner nature, in the outside world and in the intimacy of the psyche. She is the rich, fertile, fecund dark energy of the body, of nature, and in human life that alchemically work for the transformation of the human life to the Divine life.

She Is the Queen of Earth:

The Black Madonna, as is the historical Mary, is known as the suffering woman, the "La Donna Bruchetta," the burned virgin or maiden. Harvey asserts that she is the appearance of a burned woman standing and enduring with dignity the flames of torture, humiliation, torment, and suffering, wearing the scars of her ordeal across her face. She stands blackened and scarred as a symbol of the pain She carries for us because of all the violations of the laws of the heart that have occurred in humankind, the death of her son, which She witnessed, and lastly, She stands for the desecration of the feminine which has taken place throughout history. She knows of the abuse that has been visited on the "feminine aspect of humankind," and the subtle and not so subtle torture that this "feminine aspect of humankind" has had to endure because of being ignored by a society that holds, in such esteem, a patriarchal mind-set.

Yet, when one dares to look closer to the mystery of her scars one finds that the burnt woman, is actually the sacred feminine on fire with love. This suffering woman is the paradox of pain and passion united. For in her wisdom she knows that it is the pain and passion—the passion and pain united—that births the new creation.

Luminous Darkness, Birther, Mystery, Alchemical Transformer of human to Divine, Scarred Feminine, the Burned Virgin—the Black Madonna is the fullness of the three universal Marys in one archetype.

Personally, I have found that Her darkness is a sign of ripeness, revealing that She is ready to be plucked and eaten, appropriated to one's being at a cellular level. Meditating on Her will allow this to happen. She will initiate you to the Cosmic Consciousness, where She will invite you to the deeper mysteries of how to birth and embody your Inner Christ, the Divine Child desiring to be born in you. But this birth takes a naked courage of willingness, for it is a Child that is born not just of a Divine Father, but also of the Divine Mother, the both/and, realized!

Since turning my inner attention to the Black Madonna, I have been blessed with a new awareness of Her Presence filling me and transforming my heart to a burning bed of radiant fire, a consuming fire that continually burns away deeper levels of the accumulated dross of materiality and attachment. It is from a consciousness of surrender and humility that I give thanks to my friend Andrew Harvey and to the Black Madonna. I willingly accept the call to assist with heralding and birthing the full return of the Sacred Feminine.

Mary Magdalene and the Black Madonna: Is There a Relationship between the Two?

"Black Madonnas are Christian borrowings from earlier...art forms that depicted Ceres, Demeter Melania, Diana, Isis, Cybele, Artemis, or Rhea as black, the color characteristic of goddesses of the Earth's fertility."
—L. Moss and S. Cappanari: *In Quest of the Black Virgin: She is Black Because She is Black*

The color black refers to the hidden and the unknown, in the later mystery schools; Mary Magdalene represented the divine feminine, with this description. This is why I associate Mary Magdalene with the Black Madonna; they both are very powerful images in their own right, yet their true roles have been hidden and obscured throughout the centuries.

Although Mary Magdalene is venerated by the Catholic Church as a saint, with a feast day dedicated to her on July 22, very little is really known about her and the role She played in the life and teachings of Jesus. She is mentioned a few times in the Canonical Gospels, but her descriptions seem fragmented and the details seem to have been shrouded or veiled. One must dig deep to gather together her whole story.

Mary Magdalene's name in Hebrew, Magdola, means "elevated" or "watchtower" and "stronghold." She was apparently a woman of immense power for that day and age, considering the culture. Mary Magdalene had to be considered powerful by some, for when She is mentioned in the Christian Gospels as one of the women accompanying Jesus—six out of seven times—She is mentioned first. This certainly connotes that in someone's opinion, She held power within the group. What power Mary Magdalene held, as fact, has never been uncovered; it has only been conjectured. One thing is true, however. Mary Magdalene was one of the devoted followers of Jesus. She was definitely a part of his inner circle.

Here are a few Biblical scriptures that speak of her power and authority:

There is only one story of an actual anointing of Jesus recorded in the Canonical Gospels. A woman at a banquet in Bethany who was said to be Mary Magdalene did it. (Refer to Luke 10:30, John 12, Mark 14:9, and Mark 26:13). In Mark 14:8, Jesus said, "She has anointed me in preparation for my burial." In the first part of Mark 14, it states, "She also came to the tomb to anoint the body." The book of John states that this person is Mary Magdalene.

Throughout the centuries, it has been intimated that Mary Magdalene was the prostitute from who Jesus cast out the demons. However, it is important to know that Mark 16:9–20, which creates the relationship between Mary Magdalene and the prostitute, was added to the manuscript of Mark at a much later date. The two most reliable and earlier manuscripts of Mark did not have 16:9–20, they end with 16:8. Biblical scholars are aware that Mark 16:9–20 was added much later, due to papal direction and influence.

Margaret Starbird, in *The Goddess in the Gospels,* reflects on Mary Magdalene as ***"the incarnation of 'Hagia Sophia'...Holy wisdom. She was the archetypal Sister–Bride and Beloved of Jesus, his 'mirror' image in the feminine."*** She goes on to say that during the thirteenth century many ***"important epithets that once belonged to the Magdalene were shifted to the Blessed Virgin Mary."*** Why? One has to begin to ask this question at some point. Perhaps the following will help to shed some light on this.

In the Nag Hammadi Library texts (found in Egypt in 1945 but written shortly after Christ's death), Mary Magdalene is given great importance and stature among Jesus' followers. It is even hinted at in these Gospels that perhaps there was a conjugal relationship between Jesus and Mary Magdalene. In the Gospel of Phillip it states, "Jesus loved Mary Magdalene more than all the disciples and used to kiss her often on the mouth."

In several of the Gnostic Gospels, Mary Magdalene is portrayed as a woman filled with the wisdom of the Holy Spirit. These Gospels also refer to the idea that Jesus instructed Mary Magdalene in the wisdom of the "hidden teachings." In the Dialogue of the Savior, Jesus praises Mary Magdalene for her willingness to learn and for the wisdom she reveals. This accolade or acceptance by Jesus occurs much to the dismay of Peter, for when he is informed that Jesus has bestowed this admiration on Mary Magdalene, a woman, Peter outwardly displays his disdain and jealousy toward her.

The Nag Hammadi texts also refer to God as Mother and mention James and Mary Magdalene as two of the disciples that shared this sacred message. The Gnostics, the authors of this library, centered their group in Alexandria, Egypt. Their belief system taught that because of the inherent feminine nature of the Divine, everyone has direct access to God; thus a woman is equal to a man and can participate in leadership roles within the community.

Can you imagine how frightening these writings were (and still are) for the church that had been started under the patriarchal rules and dogma of Peter and Paul? No wonder in the third century C.E., the church burned and/or abolished everything that the Gnostics had to say and with it, everything that was associated with the relationship of Mary Magdalene and Jesus.

I find it very interesting that the Nag Hammadi Library would be found the same year that the first atomic bomb was dropped 1945. To me, it seems that 1945 opened the door of consciousness to new ideas through several happenings. They include the following:

1. The dropping of the first atomic bomb invoked a universal emotional (a feminine attribute) wake-up call. It heralded a need for humankind to make a decision to change its course of thinking/consciousness or risk destroying the world.
2. The beginning of the baby-boom explosion resulting in a massive entry of "old" souls with a new level of consciousness that was not willing to accept the "old" patriarchal status quo.
3. The finding of the Gnostic Gospels and all of the "new" (and feminine-oriented) revelations they would bring forth, such as:

   a. The revealing of God in a feminine aspect, The Mother along with The Father, the two as One;

   b. Alluding to the idea that Jesus perhaps had a more "human" or normal lifestyle than had previously been known; that perhaps he was not celibate but was indeed married—as was the Jewish custom—to Mary Magdalene;

   c. The revealing of Jesus' willingness to teach the "hidden manna" or deeper messages to both male and female alike, not just his chosen male disciples; the message that Divinity is found within. (I would venture to say that this was scary for the first century church, which was being organized, for what need would there be for a hierarchy or priestly intervention if one knew that everything he needed was within?); and

   d. The revelation that Mary Magdalene (a woman) played a much larger part within the society than had been previously known. She appears to be one of the principal players who held a leadership position within the group. All of these "feminine-oriented realities" began to come to light during the same year.

Is all this just a coincidence or is something greater at work here?

The Journey Is Not Always an Easy One

"Diminishing and dying are as essential as becoming. The Black Madonna beckons one to such an unorthodox understanding, even if unconsciously. That is why so many people make pilgrimages to her yearly. She does not fight the knowledge of the Father. She offers a wisdom of her own, which is experienced in the depths of the psyche."

—Esther Harding: *Women's Mysteries*

Have you ever, because of the painful experiences going on in your life, felt like you were in the midst of dying? Yet, somewhere deep within you, a silent call kept sounding its echo throughout your being. And the sound that seemed to be resounding throughout your being was saying something like this: "This is a test. You are not alone; you will get through this!"

Or perhaps you have awakened from a dream with a feeling, a remembering that a dark-skinned woman had been whispering Her secrets in your ear. These haunting siren calls heard in the depth of your being, just may have been the archetypal feminine desiring to make Her presence known to you. She is known to appear when the student is ready; when somewhere deep in the recesses of your soul you have said, "Yes, I desire to be changed."

This archetypal feminine only offers Her gifts to those who will acknowledge Her presence. She comes to both men and women alike. She does not discriminate based on gender. Through Her cycles of death and rebirth, She asks us to not only face our deepest insecurities, but to also transcend them. To walk with Her, we must be willing to dance with birth, death and rebirth, to accept the cycles of life, change, and transformation.

The dark-skinned goddess takes one's acknowledgment of Her seriously, for She knows that to be a devotee requires a responsibility to work with the changes that She guides one to. When the dark goddess beckons and the call is answered, She begins the alchemical transforming process that ultimately leads to being changed at depth. She starts this process by asking us to enter the mysterious unknown, the luminous darkness. She knows that in saying yes to sitting in the midst of this darkness, one will be transformed; for in the midst of this sacred darkness is a fire.

China Galland, in *Longing for Darkness,* speaks of the dark Madonna, her fire and her blackness in this way: ***"The Madonna is black for She enters lives as fire,"*** to which can be added; feminine energy in It's various forms (e.g., the Black Madonna) enters a person's life as fire in order to burn off the dross, the negative, the undesirable aspects of the little self. It is these negative aspects that keep us from living our wholeness and knowing our oneness with the universe and all others. The sacred fire is also known as the fire of transmutation, the alchemical transformer. In this role as the fire-keeper, the dark goddess is the redeeming aspect of darkness, the Alchemical Feminine.

The Black Madonna's (and all the archetypal dark goddess'), darkness and fire consumes the walls of insecurity that we have built in order to try to protect ourselves. The burning off of the dross and the destruction of the self-created artificial barriers (a.k.a., control, manipulation, the need to be right, unworthiness, and jealousy) require an ultimate meltdown in order to release us from our self-imposed mental and emotional prisons. The meltdown of these barriers requires that we come face to face with our deepest fears and insecurities.

With the barriers down, we are forced to stand in "nakedness" in front of the mirror of life and assess the image that we see reflected to us. Naked in front of this mirror of life, personality lumps, bumps, and flaws are revealed. We cannot hide from them. These are the fears that we have kept hidden by the clothes of conditioning. This uncovering requires an honest review of us—of the situations and the conditions of our lives. In this state of total vulnerability we are called to make a decision about what we see and to choose consciously what it is that we will do now. Will we stay as we are or change and rid ourselves of outdated and outmoded ways of being?

This energy of the feminine, especially in the form of the dark goddess is powerful. She rids us of those thoughts, beliefs and ideas that are no longer of value in our lives. In the beginning, we see this removal of the old, not for what it is, but as uncontrollable chaos in our lives. We do not recognize that this *perceived* chaos is a part of a greater Divine picture. We resist and fight the energy of change and do not understand why it is happening.

We become frustrated by the events of life and try to control them without much success. What the energy of the dark goddess reveals to us, once we are willing to acknowledge her, is that inherent in all the experiences of life is this aspect of birth, death and rebirth. She teaches us that these energies are as much a part of life as breathing—and so is She and Her darkness.

The archetypal energy of transformation and change that the feminine and the dark goddesses stand for is held in the consciousness of the matrix of creation. Held as an agent for the movement of life, life cannot be in a state of status quo but always must be in a dynamic flow of change, transformation, and transmutation; that is life's nature.

If this premise of change as a constant of life is true, then the question of life **is not,** "**Why** is this happening to me?" **but** "**What** can I learn from this experience?" Regardless of the appearance, the true work of the sacred darkness is to lead us through the so-called fires to a greater sense of our true reality. It requires that we hold a deeper understanding of the idea that that which appears to be lost, is just a steppingstone to that which is waiting to be gained. This new sense of reality contains a clearer sense of our value as sacred human beings and the sacred value of others as well.

The journey with Her is not always an easy one. To walk with the archetypal feminine energies, one must be willing to dance with birth, death, and rebirth; the cycles of life, of change, and transformation. Her call to change is as constant as the cycles of the seasons. But those who have been willing to make the journey have found that it always concludes with their being changed at depth, transformed at their core, having gained a sense of new-found wisdom. Ultimately, Her pilgrims realize that the path they traverse with Her is one they will always cherish.

Through Her cycles of death and rebirth, She does not ask us just to face our deepest insecurities, but also to uplift them. Facing the cycles ends up being the easy part. Incorporating their lessons into our lives is a more difficult task. For we must give up being a victim if we want to incorporate Her teachings into dynamic self-change.

Moving into a willingness to change our deepest fears and insecurities requires bravery, determination, and utmost trust. She does, however, know that on the other side of the pain, chaos, and destruction lies the ability to emerge as a Wise One (a.k.a., an enlightened being, a Christ, a Bodhisattva, one who knows that they don't know—and knows that it is all right.).

A Madonna Moment

Thealogy—No, It Is Not a Typo

There are writings from scholars with a feminist bent who speak of *Thealogy* instead of *Theology. Theology* means the study of God—honoring a masculine-oriented sacred Being. *Thealogy* is the study of religion, which honors a feminine Godhead. Sometimes in referring to The Black Madonna, I use only the initials T.B.M. During meditation a set of words for T.B.M. came to me:

Thealogy Breakthrough Mysticism

To me these words had the following meanings:

As *theology* is the study of our traditional patriarchal Godhead, ***Thealogy*** would be the study of ideas around a matriarchal Godhead. Thealogy seems to be a natural fit here because The Black Madonna is an aspect of the feminine nature of the Divine and we are conducting a study of her in that role.

Breakthrough stands for the gifts the Black Madonna gives us—the transformational insights that break down self-imposed barriers of negative thoughts and beliefs. The Black Madonna, as an aspect of the archetypal energy of the feminine nature of the Divine, is a carrier of the energy for transformation and change.

Mysticism means a direct experience with the Divine without any human intercessors and She certainly has the capacity for that. The Black Madonna has come to many, my self included, who did not have any idea of who She was or what She stood for, and Her influence and presence in their lives has changed them at depth.

Therefore, ***Thealogy Breakthrough Mysticism*** seems to express in a few words those ideals that the Black Madonna encompasses.

PART II

HOW TO DEVELOP A RELATIONSHIP WITH THE ALCHEMICAL FEMININE ARCHETYPES

"Inherent in the energies of the archetypal feminine
and the Black Madonna
is the ability to light fires, to move status quo
and to birth new awareness'."
—T.G.B.

Deepening the Sacred Connection

Perhaps the archetypal feminine, in the form of the Divine Mother, the Black Madonna or one of the many dark goddesses has touched your life already or maybe you would like them to but you don't know what to do to develop the relationship. You can do several elementary things to create and/or deepen your sacred connection with the archetypal feminine forces::

—Open Your Heart: Believe that the archetypal energies (of the Divine Mother, the Black Madonna and so forth) have the ability to help you; open your heart to the existence and activity of a Feminine nature of the Divine and to the archetypal energy of the Feminine. Trust that the Divine Mother is everywhere present and is just as available as the Divine Father. Seek Her in the ancient myths and stories of the goddesses and in the various religious traditions (Hindu, Buddhist, Taoist, Christian, Islamic, Native American).

—Invoke the presence of the archetypes that you resonant with and speak to them as you would a friend; call on them as you would a friend. Once you are familiar with the individual gifts and virtues they bestow, ask them for guidance. They are archetypal energy and that energy lives in our consciousness matrix and is everywhere present. The archetypal energy that they hold and which you can call forth to work with every day includes the energy of willpower, empowerment, healing, transformation, protection, leadership, discernment, love, wisdom, creativity, endurance, mystery, and communication, to name a few.

—Create sacred space (an altar) and invite them into your home; create a space to honor the sacred. Situate the altar in an area where others will not disturb it. This is your sacred space. (See the section on How to Create Sacred Space in Your Home or Workplace, page __.)

—Meditate daily, spend a few minutes each day meditating on Her sacred gifts; this helps to build the energy and to call Her energy forth.

—Incubate a relationship through your dreams; invite Her presence to be with you in your dreams. (See the section on Dream–Incubation, page __.)

—Read Her stories and myths; discover the specific strengths and gifts that each feminine archetype has to bestow. Many God-dess stories are ancient myths much older than the Bible. Many of these myths contain the same type of stories and lessons as those contained in the traditional Hebrew and Christian sacred writings. Read them, you might be surprised at what they contain!

How to Create Sacred Space in Your Home or Workplace

Purpose: To create a space that you honor and hold as sacred.

Materials: A small table, candle, sacred pictures, sacred objects, or anything else that calls to you.

Creating a sacred space or altar in your home or workplace. Situate the space in an area where others will not disturb it. This is your sacred space. Consecrate and dedicate the space to the intention that it holds special energy and meaning for you. (You may want to use the exercise, ***An Invocation for Creating Sacred Space,*** on next page.)

Place items on this altar that have meaning to you. These can be items such as sacred pictures that speak to your heart, colored candles, natural rocks from places you have visited, symbolic representations of the elements, and the energy of the four directions.

You may want to place a container of water or essential oil on it—the water/oil gathers the energy of the sacred experiences you have at the altar. Then when you are going to celebrate a special occasion, you can use the blessed water/oil in the ceremony.

You can do something very special during times of ritual and blessing, placing food offerings on your altar, letting the food be blessed by the energy there. In the Hindu culture, this blessed food is known as Prasad. To eat Prasad that the guru has blessed is considered a blessing for the one ingesting it. Prasad should be eaten slowly and with reverence.

Spend a few minutes a day in the quiet, in prayer and/or meditating at your altar. This helps to build and maintain the energy in the space around it. As you build the energy, you will find that you will be able to enter a deeper state of meditation, more quickly and easily.

An Invocation for Creating Sacred Space

Always remember—the place on which you stand is holy ground!

Turn and face each of the directions listed below and speak the words in the corresponding list.

EAST	SOUTH	WEST	NORTH
Spring	**Summer**	**Autumn**	**Winter**
Air	**Fire**	**Water**	**Earth**
March wind	**Flame of change**	**River's flow**	**Gravity's pull**
Morning's song	**Heat of passion**	**Font of feelings**	**Ground of being**
Earth's breath	**Kundalini**	**Interactive bonds**	**Mystery**
Birth	**Youth**	**Middle age**	**Wisdom Time**
Dawn	**Noon's sun**	**Evening**	**Night**
Thinking	**Intuition**	**Feeling/emotion**	**Sensation**
Mind	**Revealer-Inner Self**	**Cycles/blessings**	**Root of life**
Soul	**Spirit**	**Illusions**	**Body**
White/gold	**Red/orange**	**Blue-green/Silver**	**Earth tones**
Marshmallows	**Cinnamon**	**Water**	**Nuts/grain**
Raphael	**Michael**	**Gabriel**	**Uriel**
Healing words	**Vision/Glad tidings**	**Purification/Truth**	**Wisdom**
Sword	**Wand**	**Cup**	**Disk**
Persephone and Artemis: New Beginnings	**Pele and Kali: the Power to Destroy and Heal**	**Demeter and Kuan Yin: Love manifest**	**Mother Earth/Gaia /Hecate: Matter**
Welcome Energies of the East	**Welcome Energies of the South**	**Welcome Energies of the West**	**Welcome Energies of the North**

Return to the East: We have come full circle and we have called forth the pure essence of who we are and of what it is that we intend to establish in this sacred space. We understand that Essence is the completion; coming full circle; the energy permeating all; wholeness; Unity; relating to all the elements; balance; harmony; the circle with a dot in the center, and the dot is the bindu, the point of origin and return.

Ending: ***"By the air that is her breath"***
"By the water that is her womb"
"By the fire that is her spirit"
"By the Earth that is her body"
"By the energy permeating all, we/I declare this sacred space."

Entering a Sacred Site: A Ceremony for Pilgrimages and Journeys (Adapted author unknown)

If you are fortunate enough to have the opportunity to visit the shrine of a Black Madonna or an ancient site where the Madonna or Divine Mother has been venerated (in what ever form She has taken), I would invite you to use the following practice prior to entering the grounds. I have listed for you earlier in the book several names of the sites (and the countries) that are considered to be carriers of Her energy.

The Ceremony for Pilgrimages and Journeys: Calling Forth Sacred Energy

When you say "yes" to visiting a sacred site or power place the experience can have a very healing effect on you spiritually, physically, emotionally, and mentally. A sacred space is said to be a place where the Earth interacts with the psyche of the person visiting, meaning that the space has an energy that is palpable and is actually interacting with the person standing within it. This is not an intellectual experience but a deep cellular feeling that connects one to the energy and the Earth of the space.

This is thought to occur because the Earth and stones are a witness to that which has occurred in this place. In other words, they hold the energy, the sacredness of the space. The wisdom, energy, and harmony interpenetrating the Earth and stones at a site, especially an ancient site, can "Bring to alignment the perception of a fragmented spirit, soul, and body."

In order to receive the most from these earthly power points, the following are a few ideas to incorporate to your pilgrimage experience:

- First acknowledge that you are intending to take a pilgrimage, a sacred journey in order to know yourself in a deeper way. Go with the expectation of receiving a gift from the energy inherent in each site you will visit. Yet be willing to release any preconceived notion of what the journey should look like and what you should feel as you enter the site. Be willing to sit in the center of the unknown.
- Prior to visiting the site, select a prayer, angel card, scripture, or sacred writing; let it set the stage for your visit. Doing this will help you to create a deeper sense of intentionality in your interaction with the energy of the site.
- While you are approaching the site—stay alert. Let the energy of the each site you visit begin to speak to you visually and psychically. While you are still at a distance from the site, observe its shape. How do you relate to its shape? Consider it both visually and from your feeling nature. Does it make you feel at peace or upset you in some way? Does it elicit in you a

sense of awe? Do you feel dominated by its grandeur? Does it remind you of anything going on in your life? What is your body saying to you?

- What do you observe around the area of the site? Streams? Hills? Houses? Countryside? Mountains? Water? Valleys? Lakes? Ponds? Wells? Observe their shapes; think about what it is that their shapes remind you of.
- As you enter the site, stop and consciously begin to breathe its air. Exhale the air in your lungs and then inhale afresh. Consciously intend to partake of the energy of the site. Do this several times.
- After this, honor the energy in the space and begin to create a relationship with it. Expressing yourself in an honest, simple way, state your intention for being there.

"I acknowledge the sacred energy contained within this space. I have come to unite with this sacred energy and to learn from its wisdom!"

- Wait for an internal response (a feeling, a chill, a knowing).
- Consciously open your awareness to your six senses—look, listen, feel, touch, smell, and intuit your surroundings. Be aware of what you are bringing to the moment. Be aware of everything around you. Watch how the sunlight moves across the landscape (walls, ceilings, water, hills). Listen for any sounds of birds singing, the wind howling, animals wailing in the background, all vying for your attention in a subtle way. Feel the energy of the place. Touch that which is appropriate. Lie down on a rock and get a sense of its message. Interact consciously!
- Ask for guidance and listen interiorly. Do not negate what comes forth. Be willing to interact with your instincts. If your heart tells you to sing, start to chant. If it says pray, then stop and pray. If you begin to cry, let the tears roll forth. Take your time, walk around, and absorb the energy.
- As you are ready to leave, give thanks for the gift you have received from interacting with the sacred energies of the space.
- After leaving the space, go to a quiet place and journal your thoughts and feelings.

Dream–Incubation

"The Black Madonna repeatedly appears in modern dreams, and her presence suggests the possibility of a feminine consciousness as yet unknown to us. Her coming presages a new understanding"
—Marion Woodman: *The Ravaged Bridegroom: Masculinity in Women*

"Was I dreaming?" "Were you there?' "Who are you and what do you want from me?" If you desire to enhance your relationship or begin a relationship with one of the dark goddesses, dream-incubation is a tool you can use. Night is the playground of the Black Madonna and dark goddesses and often their first appearance is in a dream. On awakening, you will recall that a dark-skinned woman appeared in your dream; perhaps she was offering you a gift or telling you something that seemed apropos to the situation you were in the midst of.

Dreams are said to be the mysterious language of the night. They are thought to be both the conscious mind releasing stress and the unconscious mind calling forth the future, remembering the past, answering your questions, reminding you of who you are as a spiritual Being, sending you messages of warning or good, taking you to "other lands," and providing healing on all levels of awareness. Dreams are tools you can use to discover your truth. Dreamtime is productive time. It is believed that 20 percent of your sleep is spent in dreaming (about one and a half hours per night). Dreaming is as natural to you as eating.

The famous psychiatrist Dr. Carl Jung referred to dreams as ways to delve to the collective unconscious that stores all the beliefs and wisdom common to all cultures and societies. The collective unconscious contains common archetypal symbols and metaphors and is said to be the realm of our "ancestral memories." The collective unconscious contains a symbolic language that, once decoded, is familiar to all, regardless of geographical location or culture. I personally prefer to describe dreams as metaphorical portraits, pictures that my Higher Self paints in order that I might come to learn more about myself.

When you awaken in the morning with a particularly clear memory of a dream, I believe this clarity is a signal that there is something in you, a message of sorts, that is trying to make itself known. Here is a simplistic overview of how the dream world works: the left hemisphere of your brain holds the rational, logical, analytical, masculine aspect of your being and is aligned with your conscious mind. The left brain is alert when you are awake. It holds the personality side of you and is the dominant processor of your information. However, when you sleep, you change information processors from the left hemisphere to the right hemisphere of the brain. The right hemisphere of the brain holds the creative, intuitive, abstract, feminine aspect of your being and is aligned with and holds the information of your unconscious/subconscious mind. Your right brain stays quite alert while you are sleeping and has the skills which function best in "the metaphorical landscape of dreams."

In your right brain, during sleep time, you are more closely connected to your Higher Presence than at any other time during the day. It is through this right brain sleep connection that your Higher Presence tries to communicate to you. But this Higher Self will not necessarily communicate with you directly; it prefers to use coded messages, codes such as symbols, metaphors, and archetypes. Your Higher Self or Presence tries to open the way for you to participate in transformation and change, but It will not force you. No! It is much subtler than that. I believe the reason The Higher Self uses this subtle route of messaging is that you have been given freewill by the Creator and even though you are ready to make changes, you must choose both on your soul level and conscious level in order to do so.

Think about the right hemisphere of your brain as akin to a relay station that sends information from your Higher Self to your physical personality (which is governed by the left brain or masculine aspect). When you sleep, dream information from the subconscious realm of your being passes through your right brain. On waking, the left brain analyzes the dream information that has been received to see if it can be understood from its current frame of reference, which is logic, reason, science, rationality, If the left brain has a reference point, you will be able to decode and understand the message and receive the proverbial Aha! If there is not a reference point, the left brain will dismiss the message and you will lose this opportunity to gain insight about your self and your world.

Therefore, the clearer your concepts are around dreams, the greater your understanding is and the more skill you acquire in interpreting your dreams and their symbolic language of metaphor and archetypes; the greater will be the potential for you to uncover your deepest fears, to live in balance and learn to understand yourself at every level of your Being—physical, mental, emotional, and spiritual.

Many times when a person is ready on a soul level to make a change in his or her life, the first clue will come from dreams. One of the archetypes, such as the Black Madonna, will reveal Herself with a coded message about the change or other symbolic images may come forth which have universal meaning, such as a house being flooded, crossing a river, your sight being restored, and so forth. When you more fully understand these messages you will see what great tools they are for opening you to greater potential and for deciphering the messages of inner spiritual awareness.

But before a person can understand about the symbolic images that come forth in dreams, it is important to have a clear picture about how information gets deposited in the subconscious mind. Let's begin with a few questions to see how much you know about the development of our belief systems and their effect on us as adults.

Where did the original perceptions that you hold about who you are as a person come from? How was your belief system created? How do your childhood experiences affect you as an adult? How, then, are these perceptions or beliefs translated to symbolic figures that show up in your dreams?

Here is the answer in one simplistic scenario. (Please feel free to change the details to fit your specific situation/s; the results will be the same.)

Imagine that you are a young child who is overweight. You are the brunt of many jokes. Your parents and siblings continually tease you about being fat. Over and over they poke fun at you and call you "Tubby." You hate this teasing, you hate being called "Tubby," and you hate being fat. Over the years, as the teasing continues, you get angrier and it hurts more and more. Every time someone says "that" word to you, you cringe; an emotional response is elicited even if you become adept at hiding it.

Now you are an adult and you are actually as skinny as a rail, but every time you look at yourself in a mirror you see yourself as fat. You carry this picture of that kid in your mind; the image makes you want to continue to "diet" beyond what others perceive as healthful. But you are compelled by an uncontrollable urge from within to become even skinnier. This leads you to start taking other measures, such as engaging in bulimic activities like forced vomiting. You hate this behavior, but you cannot seem to stop it. You are becoming distraught. You desire to change, but you can't or something inside won't let you.

One morning you wake up and realize that you have just had a very strange dream. As you recall the details, you remember that this is not the first time that this dream has occurred. In the dream, a dark-skinned woman comes to you holding a balloon. She tells you that the balloon has a gift for you, but you must discover what its gift is. She hands the balloon to you and as soon as you take it, the balloon begins to grow bigger and bigger until it finally explodes. As it explodes, it scatters everywhere, leaving you holding nothing. (Remember, the right brain is the holding area for the images pertaining to your body.)

These dreams are so vivid that you decide to go to someone to help you interpret the symbolism of the dreams. Through therapeutic dream analysis sessions you gradually come to the realization that the balloon is an unconscious symbol that is reflecting your waking reality. The balloon represents the belief that you hold about your body image. It is telling you that your belief that you are as "fat as a pig" is getting bigger and bigger and will "explode" or kill you if you do not begin to make significant changes in your life.

You come to find out this has happened because that little "fat kid" in you who was continually teased still lives as a belief system in your subconscious and continues to haunt you. You choose to begin to take steps to heal your past. (Hidden, unhealed belief systems are the root cause for many who suffer from addictive disorders, alcoholism, anorexia, or bulimia.)

The perceptions you hold about who you believe you were and who you still are were developed or imprinted to your subconscious through the positive and negative experiences that have occurred throughout your life.

How this imprinting works is like this: every time a situation comes up and you get hurt, get angry, are made sad or happy, there is elicited an energetic emotional response, which is either positive or negative depending on your perception of the situation or incidence. All these experiences have accumulated over time and formed energetic thought messages.

When enough energy is gathered around a particular message, it gets stored at the subconscious level (and cellular level of your body). As these energetic thought messages gather together they begin to form the essence of your belief system and core values.

These beliefs are stored memories in your subconscious mind and have created the perceptions that you now carry regarding your body image, your self-image, your worth as a person, your ultimate value in society, your value within your professional career, your family system, and what you truly think you deserve from life.

The positive perceptions, it goes without saying, helped you. But the negative perceptions, unless you have consciously worked to make changes in your belief system, remain and create havoc in your life, for they hold an energetic trigger within them. The trigger is a behavioral or emotional response that is conditioned to your system and when you perceive that you are about to lose control or be demeaned, you move to a protective response, which is usually one that is unconscious and unflattering to you. You carry these hidden messages (triggers) in your subconscious mind (the subconscious realm) and they rear their heads—usually in the form of a "shadow-type" behavior causing negative effects in your life.

This is why it is important to understand your dreams, for they are your connection to the subconscious realm of mind. When you are ready to make changes in your life, often you will be made aware of this desire to change through a dreams or a series of dreams. Symbolic images will come forth in your dreams and when you can understand what it is that these messages are trying to tell you, you will see what great tools they are for opening you to greater potential and for deciphering the message from your inner spiritual awareness, your Higher Self.

It is also important to know that if you continually ignore the dream messages, which are coming from your deeper soul level (a.k.a., Higher Self, right hemisphere), about your need to change, often the right brain will try another route to get your attention. It will begin to communicate its message directly through the body itself in the form of discomfort or dis-ease. Remember, the right brain works in the arena of symbols, so what it will do is create a symbolic dis-ease within the body to get its message noticed.

You are continually late paying bills and stay in massive debt. You don't like yourself for being like this and you know you should change, and you want to, but you don't. However, lately you have noticed that on waking each morning you are recalling the dream that you had that night. Each dream over the last few days has had a common theme: there was a mess you had to clean up. Each dream that you have recalled contained instances of flooding, large spills, trucks overturned, and you were left alone to take care of all the clean-up.

However, since the dream world means nothing to, you pay no attention to these dreams. Suddenly you begin to suffer from lower back pain, which is the energetic home in the body of messages regarding finances and order. Get the connection? Your body, through your dreams, is trying to tell you that you have an issue. But you ignore both the dream and the problem. So your Higher Self mind, not being able to change you through your dreams, takes another step to try to change you; it affects your body in order to get your attention. Energetically your body will let you know when you are out of step with the greater path for your life. The question is always, will you listen now or later?

I would venture to say if you were to be totally honest with yourself, that before any illness has made itself known in your body, you had presenting signs telling you that there was something in your life that needed to change and you ignored all the signs. You were probably warned symbolically in your dreams for a long time prior to the illness that it was time to make a change in your lifestyle.

In the Christian Bible there are twenty-two references to receiving guidance through dreams. The art of dream incubation is thought to have originated in ancient Greece. In fact, dream work became so popular that 300 to 400 dream temples were built in Greece in honor of the god Aesclepias. The temples in Greece were said to be active for more than a thousand years, starting at the end of the sixth century B.C.E. Dream weavers or seekers would go to these temples for the purpose of receiving a useful dream or prophecy from a god. They believed that by sleeping in a holy place that had been dedicated to a specific purpose and to a dream god, they would receive the answers to their questions. It has been found that other cultures such as the Chinese, Japanese, Egyptians, Hebrews, Maltese, and more also used dream incubation.

Dream incubation is a process by which you select a dream topic and then program yourself into it. You can incubate dreams just as a bird incubates eggs to allow them to come to birth. You can direct your dreams by consciously intending to do so. Dream incubation is a concept that says you consciously guide the course of your dreams from the wakeful state. Therefore, if you desire to call forth energy of one of the archetypal Black Madonnas, here is what you do:

Guidelines for Dream Incubation

1. Honor your sleep-space as a sacred temple of dream incubation, e.g., light a candle prior to starting the dream incubation process. Play soft music, burn incense, do whatever you are guided to do to call forth a sense of sacredness in your space. (Prior to falling asleep blow out the candle.)
2. Choose a time when you are not too tired and have not used drugs or alcohol.
3. Intend to set aside plenty of time in the morning to process the information you receive during the night.
4. Place a journal and pen or tape recorder beside your bed. You are setting the stage in order that on arising you can recall all the details of your dreams and make notes of them.
5. Trust that your Higher Self already knows what you need. Trust that the information that is going to be revealed is part of your solution. Even if it does not seem to make sense when you awaken, it will make sense in time.
6. Decide on the subject or issue you desire to incubate. Calling forth the Black Madonna and the special message she has for you is the important action.
7. Then contemplate the specific issue. Get in touch with your feelings and emotions around the issue. Have a clear intention and your dreams will respond, e.g., if you desire to know the Black Madonna, find a picture of her and any information you can find, then sit with her picture and think about her. What do you want from her? What if she really gives it to you? What will you do? How will your life change?
8. Ask yourself: "Am I really willing to have this issue resolved? Am I willing to let it go? How would my life be different if that problem were solved?" "Am I really willing to meet the Black Madonna and follow her guidance?" We must be willing to release in order to receive.
9. Before falling asleep, state your request several times. "Help me know and understand the Black Madonna and my fear of the darkness." Let go of any distractions that may come up. Continue to return to the question.
10. Try to keep your spine straight as you sleep.
11. Remember to write everything down on awakening and **trust** your guidance!
12. Throughout the day answers may come to you. Have a pen and paper ready to jot down this new information, these new awarenesses.
13. Happy dreaming!

A Madonna Moment

As shared in a previous chapter, my first encounter with the archetypal divine feminine occurred in January 1990, in the form of a dream; the dream revealed itself in this manner:

The Dream: I was alone in my house, when suddenly; a dark-skinned woman appeared out of nowhere. She invited me to go on a journey with her, and then held out her hand. I accepted, took her hand and She proceeded to lead me down a flight of stairs into the basement of my home. I was surprised, for unbeknownst to me, in my basement was all kinds of equipment that I had never seen; it looked like someone was making "moonshine" whiskey.

I asked what was going on, a different dark-skinned woman, an older, not very attractive, wise woman (and there were several others there, also) informed me that they were making Miracle-Grow. The older wise woman, said that if I would be willing to stay with them, down in the basement and help them make the Miracle-Grow, the women would pay me $30,000/month. I said "yes." I would stay with them, but not for the money. I was interested in what Miracle-Grow could do for the world.

The Dream Interpretation:

*I was in my house (my soul);

*I was alone (this work can only be done by me)

*The dark skinned woman appears (the archetypal feminine);

*Out of nowhere (She is nowhere and every where at the same time);

*She invited me to go on a journey (the feminine extends an invitation to participate with Her energies, rarely does She force you to "dance" with Her);

*Extending Her hand and my taking it (I was saying "yes" to Her and what ever She had in store for me);

*Saying "yes," (was saying that this woman was someone I trusted – She was in fact, an aspect of my Higher Self);

*She led me to the basement (the subconscious realm);

*All equipment needed (everything I needed to do—the deeper work to change and transform my thoughts—was already within me);

*The "moonshine" (a symbol of the Divine Feminine is the Moon, which represents the cycles of life and transformation – a prophecy of things to come);

*The older, not very attractive, wise woman (a double message – lessons are not always wrapped in pretty packages and true beauty lives within.)

*My asking what was going on (this represented my willingness to find out what needed to be done by me);

*The Miracle-Grow (the work She and I would do together in order for me to grow me to a higher state of awareness);

*The money (the gift of the work);

*The vast sum of money (the ultimate result of participating in the work is beyond anything one can imagine);

*The fact that She was willing to pay me (the work to be done is worth whatever it takes to get through it, because the payoff in the great scheme of things, is so great);

*Saying "yes" to staying in the basement (the agreement to go forward into the Unknown and the Mystery of Her Domain);

*Doing the work, not for money but for the world (I am doing the work for the pure joy of finding the deeper essence of my self and then taking that Truth into service in the world).

PART III

BEING THE "LIVING" CHALICE

Working with Higher Dimensional Frequencies (e.g. the Energy of Feminine Archetypes) in the Process of Conscious Transformation

"A very solid cup has to be prepared to hold the increasingly burning wine of gnosis, and this solid cup can only be created in us by a desire to purify ourselves of every habit, disordered appetite and fantasy that keeps us slaves to ourselves."

—Andrew Harvey

Perfume of the Desert

"Living" Chalice Energy

"The story is stranger than fiction. It is a surprising spiritual journey, the years I spent searching for the lost Grail of the European legends, and the final realization that it was not an artifact I was searching for but..."

—Margaret Starbird

The Goddess in the Gospels

"I was searching for the Essence of myself."

—T.G.B.

"I Am a Chalice for the
Rebirth of the Divine Feminine.
I Am a Chalice of Sacred Fire."

— Priscilla Richards

Interpreting the Symbology of the Chalice from the Story of the Holy Grail

In *Brothers of the Grape*, Michael Arnold shares these words, "***The mystical meaning of the Search for the Holy Grail is man's search [desire] to find the cup of his capacity from which he can drink of life's fulfillment ...***"

A desire to know more about the symbolic meaning or mystery of the Holy Grail and yourself as a symbol of that sacred container is said to mean that you are ready to be *It*. Symbols have been used for centuries in teaching as an abstract representation of a concrete idea; and as a way to provide a hiding place for the deeper essence of a message. Symbols are important in teaching and learning because they represent steps in the masonry of the soul. They are building blocks of consciousness, for they bypass conscious mind and intellect and take the deeper essence of the lesson being presented, directly to the heart.

Symbols have been said to be "the language of the soul." They are also the language of the subconscious mind and the imagination. Consciously engaging the subconscious mind and the imagination—through the use of their common language of symbols, dreams, images, and archetypes—taps into and expands our understanding of the mystery behind all life.

The subconscious mind is the sensitive plate of the universe, imprinting all our thoughts, beliefs, values, and ideals; it does not know right or wrong; it only gives back to us what has been imprinted. Our imagination is the interior faculty that forms and shapes that which has been imprinted on the subconscious and all of life is born out of this shaping.

The choice in life is: do we allow that which is before our eyes to dictate the shaping of our beliefs or do we go within and listen for another "Voice"? Allow me to support this thought with a paraphrase of a saying from Jesus, "Only those with ears will hear the true message hidden within."

Other wise teachers throughout the centuries have also used symbols to make their heart-point: Confucius, Shakespeare, Buddha, Emerson, Thoreau, and R. Browning, each used symbols and images to more poignantly represent their thoughts and teachings, rendering them more practical and understandable, e.g., "The kingdom of heaven is like a pearl." "Release the imprisoned splendor."

Symbols are the language of the subconscious mind (which is said to be feminine in nature) and were used to hide the deeper meaning behind the Holy Grail story. The legend of the Holy Grail came to being in the twelfth and thirteenth centuries C.E. Who or what actually created the story is left for history to determine, however, Dan Brown, in *The Da Vinci Code*, says that it was the Priory de Sion. The Priory, it is thought fashioned the story as a covert way to keep alive a secret message that had been being passed down through the family of its Grand Master, Godefroi de Bouillon, since the time of Jesus.

Why the Priory de Sion did this is a long story, but let it suffice to say that it is believed that in 1199 C.E. the Priory, through its offshoot the Knights Templars, discovered documents that corroborated the secret of the family of the Grand Master, Godefroi de Bouillon. These documents are thought to depict the life of Jesus, the role of women as disciples, the divine feminine as co-creator in Creation and the way to salvation in a totally different manner than that of the Catholic Church. The collection was given the name *Sangraal*, a name that was later divided to two words, *San Greal* or Holy Grail.

The Catholic Church was totally opposed to any discussion around these documents, as their proclamation was that Jesus was the only way, and it was only through an intermediary of the church that the salvation of Jesus Christ could be obtained. In fact, it was forbidden to speak of these documents and their contents, lest you be labeled a heretic—which led to being tortured and burned at the stake. Thus, the message to keep it alive had to go underground. What better way of taking this new message underground, than creating a story with a metaphor that shares a legend of a Holy Grail. The Holy Grail/Chalice, a container that held the blood of Christ, which was carefully carried to Europe by the family of Joseph of Arimathea and also accompanied by Mary Magdalene.

Alas, as with other sacred messages that have been cloaked in secret terms and hidden meanings—for fear that some "higher" authority might hear them being repeated—after a while the deeper meaning contained within the message gets lost, repressed, and/or forgotten. What remains is a shell of a story that sounds good, but whose full meaning is no longer remembered.

In the Grail story, a detailed description of the Chalice is given. It is described as a chalice crafted of both gold and silver with jewels imbedded around the bowl and tiny pearls surrounding its rim. The Chalice description of the combination of the gold and silver was a secret metaphor for the idea that when the masculine and feminine come to a state of balance, there is an integration of Spirit and matter. The gold represents the masculine aspect and the silver is the feminine, the pearls are a symbol of perfection. When one places the sacred cup to their lips they are physically touching perfection.

As a symbol the Grail/Chalice is said to be a symbolic representation of:

*Our innate quest for Truth.

*The cup of everlasting energetic nourishment that comes from God.

*The balance of the masculine and feminine natures.

*Our body as a container for the energetic information system/energy mind centers, known in the Eastern traditions as the Chakras. The seven Chakras awaken individually and ultimately create one harmonious system of Dynamic Energy; the Holy Grail.

Chakras/Chalices/Energetic Mind-Centers
Our Energetic Information System

We (humankind) are electro-magnetic, physical bio-computers and our energetic electricity is the Breath of Spirit. In Its pure state, this Energy vibrates on the frequency of Christ Consciousness or Higher. Breathing through each one us, It lives in every cell of our being. Everyone has equal access to It and It is what all things are made of. It is at our disposal to use for living and expressing our creative potential. Thus, in reality we may look like physical beings, but in actuality we are bio-physical energetic systems, sustained and maintained by the Energy of the Universe.

Through seven major energy mind-centers, which in the Eastern tradition is known as the Chakra system, we access and harness all of the Energy we are receptive to, in the moment. These seven (or perhaps, twelve or more) major Chakras/energy mind-centers align throughout the body from the base of the spine to the top of the head. These are non-anatomical vortexes of energy, spinning wheels of fiery energetic fuel. Revolving and moving freely, these wheels are designed to be conduits for the Sacred Energy of The One; to move throughout our being to power and empower our world. Through the Energy accessed by these whirling wheels, we connect and have access to the Cosmic Substance of the Universe and the higher dimensional frequencies.

These Chakras, or as I like to call them Chalices, (seven individual Chalices awaken and create the One Chalice) have the ability to reflect our emotional, physical, and mental states of health, well-being, and our ability to love. It is our thoughts, beliefs and attitudes more than any thing else in life that block the release of the flow of vital Energy. The arrangement and alignment of the Chalices (from base of spine to crown) reminds us that we can ascend to the fullness of the Divine through the gradual integration of the lessons of the material world.

Chalices, as non-anatomical vortexes of energy/energy mind-centers, are vertically aligned from the base of the spine to the crown of the head and correspond with the following body areas:

The first Chalice (Chakra) or Root Chalice is at the base of the spine.
The second Chalice is in the space of the reproductive or pelvic area.
The third Chalice is located in the navel or solar plexus area.
The fourth Chalice is located in the heart space. This is the primary energy mind center. In order for harmony and balance to prevail throughout the human bio-energetic system, all (six) other Chalices must be in synchronous resonance with this one.
The fifth Chalice is located at the throat.
The sixth Chalice is located in the middle of the forehead and is known as the third eye.
The seventh Chalice is located at the top of the head or crown area.

These vortexes of energy, sit just outside and within the range of the physical body at what is called the etheric or unseen (non-anatomical) level of the body. Working together they craft an egg-shaped interlocking web or matrix of energetic frequencies that creates a grid of energy around us known as an auric field. Each individual auric field contains patterns of energy derived from past memories and experiences, which can be "read" by those whom are sensitive.

For example: Have you ever walked into a room in which an argument has just occurred and felt like the energy of anger was so thick that you could "cut the energy with a knife?" Or, have you ever said, "I don't know, I just didn't like her from the very first moment that I met her."

As an aside, in his book, *The Genius Frequency*[11], John J. Falone purports that not only do we have the seven energy mind-centers, that hold all the above described personal memories and information, but we also have five distinct bodies of energy (physical, mental, emotional, spiritual and etheric) and we live within nine dimensional fields of energy, in any given moment. Is it any wonder that the spiritual journey takes so long?

In addition, each of the seven Chalices is believed to have a relationship with an endocrine gland and the specific organs related to that endocrine gland. If one or more of our Chalices are blocked, the vital life force, our source of energy, will not flow freely. This blockage of energy is thought to increase the probability of our contracting a disease or illness and prevents us from resonating with higher dimensional frequencies.

Another important aspect of the Chalice, as depicted in the Grail story, is its shape which is a cup-like figure. Symbolically, the Chalice shape corresponds to the shape of the body and its energetic system. The correlation of the Chalice to the energetic system of the body is described below:

The container or bowl of the Chalice is believed to hold the upper Chakras; the seventh, sixth, and fifth, which are the energy centers that connect us to Spirit.

Where the stem of the Chalice meets, the bowl is the fourth Chakra or heart space. The heart is an important crucible, for it takes the higher dimensional frequencies of the spiritual realm and transforms them to be of service in the material world of matter. We cannot bring these higher frequencies to the material world without Love. Thus, the bowl or heart receives the energetic nourishment from God and transforms it for use in our bodies, lives, and affairs.

The flow of energy to the stem represents the movement of energy to the lower Chalices (third, second, and first). These are the energy mind centers that hold us in attachment to matter. They must be united with spirit. Spirit and matter must come together in sacred union. So the very structure of our living energy system provides us with the potential to be a "living" Chalice.

The Chalice also represents a container that holds a sacred liquid, thus, the metaphor reveals, to those who are spiritually wise that we as humans are the sacred container holding the precious liquid that is a mixture of the energetic fire of the

Holy Spirit (the Divine Mother) and the Power/Will (the Divine Father).

As you can see, the Grail story was created to protect and keep alive the multiple levels of sacred messages hidden within its symbolism during times when it was unwise, for fear of death, to verbally share the true wisdom of the Grail message.

As a spiritual practice, thinking of ourselves as a "living" Chalice is a symbolic image with a great deal of potency. Meditating on one's self as a Chalice of living energy, which is vibrant, moving, and renewing can elicit a breakthrough in awareness. Visualizing our body as the Grail or Chalice with all the energetic wheels in motion helps us embody its Truth and allows us to understand It at a deeper level.

Shiva and Shakti

Shakti (the feminine energy or principle) and Shiva (the masculine energy or principle) come from the Hindu spiritual tradition and symbolize the spiritual energy that lives in "dynamic opposition" within each of us. Spiritual seekers for several thousand years have desired to awaken these sacred energies and ultimately draw the two to Union. This Union of these two energies, Shakti and Shiva, results in a spiritual freedom known as bliss, liberation, or enlightenment. In the Eastern tradition, this form of spiritual awakening is known as Kundalini yoga.

Kundalini energy is believed to work in multiples of seven, meaning that each of the seven Chakras/Chalices has seven additional sub-layers. Therefore with forty-nine layers contained with the unfoldment process, it is not so much the question, "Is my Kundalini awakened?" but to what degree. Kundalini awakening doesn't happen at once or overnight.

The more fully the Chalices are awakened or flowing, the more spiritual energy can flow through them. This is a function of the brain cells, which register spiritual energy, experiences, and higher stimuli. With each layer or degree of awakening that occurs, the more energy is able to flow through the Chakra. The more spiritual energy (some call this energy Holy Spirit, the Divine Feminine) that flows through the field, the more it is reflected in the cells of the body (this is part of the regenerative process of spiritualizing the physical organism).

In Kundalini yoga, the energy that is initially awakened is the Shakti (the feminine) energy. Her energy is believed to be a fiery-coiled serpent at the base of the spine or Root Chakra, which lies dormant within us until there is an experience that calls forth its awakening or arousal. This awakening is known to occur in a multitude of ways, a few of which include a spontaneous arousal, through a Master's touch, through prayer and meditation, and through an active, and intentional pursuit of enlightenment. (We will discuss this again in a few pages.)

Once the Kundalini or Shakti energy, the sacred feminine energy, is activated, it begins to ascend the spiral staircase of the spine. Unwinding slowly, moving sinuously, it makes its way up through the seven Chakras. Each Chakra is awakened as a young woman waiting on the nuptial bed in anxious anticipation for the realization of her desire. Each Chakra's fiery liquid contents spill forth rising and rising, ever spiraling upward, leading on toward the desired prize of full ecstasy.

Thus the sacred liquid dances ambiguously upward throughout the seven successive wheels, creating an undulating path of spiritual energy in its wake, awakening and arousing a passion within like one has never known in the greatest of worldly pleasure, until at last the Shakti energy reaches the top of the head, where Shiva, (the prepared masculine or intellect) her consort, awaits her arrival. The desire for full Union ever grows and blossoms like corn ripening in the field. The nuptial bed of the Crown Chakra awaits consummation.

Fully ripened and ready for harvest, the Goddess Shakti unites with Shiva. The raw passion of spirituality's masculine and feminine energies combines to create "Cosmic Combustion." The fiery liquid penetrates the crown and the ultimate experience of bliss occurs. Then the two, entwined in each other's energy, rest in the space of enlightenment. The force of creativity that animates the cosmos has united with the raw power of the Unmanifested. Together they go forth to live in harmony and joy.

Combined, these two energies work together in an alchemical fashion; ***"like a pure crystal prism that controls the process whereby all seven [colors are] radiated by the energies of each of the seven [Chakras and] collectively transmuted to form the radiant white light of true purity and illumination."***[12]

As Chalices are awakened, our sense of power in the world increases. Power is not a sense of aggressive force, but a sense of knowing who we are. Carolyn Myss, in *Anatomy of the Spirit,*[13] refers to *power* as the ***"ability to regulate the life force flowing through us."*** Therefore, living in and with Power is learning to access the full potential of the vital life-energy flowing through us, right now! When we have learned how to harness this energy, we will be power-filled, ready to live our life's purpose to the fullest.

It is important to remember that when the Chalices are awakened, both the positive and negative energies and qualities that we hold in mind and body are stirred. This stirring will create a magnification of those qualities. Do not be afraid of this; the negative is coming forth to be realized and transformed (remember, seeds must die in order to be reborn and grow). The positive is coming forth to be of greater value in your life (but even the positive needs to burst forth anew).

Regardless of whether the qualities that come forth are seen as positive or negative, inner battles will occur. We will experience our own Armageddons. This is part of the inner purification process. The reason for the purification of the "negatives" seems to be obvious; we are ready to transform them. It is often the reason for the purification of the "positives" that baffles us. Our positive qualities can hold us back just as equally as our perceived negative ones. The positive has the ability to trap us to believe we are "the spiritually selected" or that we have all the answers for others and ourselves. It can lead to our believing that we have special powers and to using those powers in ways that are not for our highest and best, nor for the highest and best of others.

To awaken Kundalini safely, we must properly prepare the mind and body.

When Kundalini is awakened by the uninitiated or through processes that are meant to "speed up" or bypass spiritual processes, there is a potential to activate the lower natures inherent within the areas of the lower Chalices. This stimulation can increase the desire for material things or create an excessive increase in the sexual appetite. Often the uninitiated do not recognize this and that is why so many "guru-types" are now being exposed because of sex scandals.

I believe that proper purification is essential, for consciously releasing negative vices creates a solid foundation that develops inner strength. Metaphysically, "strength" is that which builds the spiritual characteristics of integrity, honesty, reliability, veracity, and harmlessness. Having the foundation of these "inner strengths" built through purification permits spiritual energy, when awakened, to flow smoothly throughout the Chalices without any blockage and without being harmful in any way to the physical body. Remember, spiritual energy is a mighty force so we do not want to short-cut or bypass the step-by-step processes needed for right awakening. Out of proper and well-defined purification processes spiritual emergence is birthed; short-cuts have the potential to lead to spiritual emergencies.

Inherent in this awakening process is another important factor that has been known for eons. That is the importance of the relationship of the head to the heart. Esoterically, it is believed that the sign of the cross made on the body is a statement that says, "Bringing the head and the heart together calls forth blessings." Therefore, before Kundalini is awakened, the heart Chalice and the Crown Chalice must be activated to work in tandem with each other. This takes time and practice. In the ancient mystery schools, it was believed that the heart is the place where inner wisdom abided; therefore, in order for an initiate to proceed on with mastery training, his intellect must be in service to heart-wisdom.

This is important because spiritual awakening enhances the capacity of the intellect, which resides in the space of Crown Chalice. Also, spiritual understanding will come under the auspices of the Crown Chalice; therefore, it is imperative that each of these two are in service to heart-wisdom and thus hold the space for harmlessness and veracity in all that is done.

The activation of this heart-crown connection then permits the free flow of spiritual energy to descend down and awaken the Kundalini energy at the base of spine, easily and safely. This is not a one-time awakening, especially if there are forty-nine degrees or levels of awakening as the Eastern Master teachers say.

I believe that the heart is the crucible of transformation for spiritual energy. It is the place where "the Mother" dances and plays in the fires of spiritual energies in Her desire to change us at depth. Through the proper regulation of the Kundalini energy, its movement up and through the higher Chalices can be smooth and less jarring to the physical system. Remember, we are talking about sacred fire, spiritual fire, and as with any fire we must honor its ability to burn and transmute.

In this same regard, it is important to know that when you work with spiritual energies, phenomena may occur; you may feel heat, cold, and pressure in your head or heart space, tingling sensations in your body, hear music, smell fragrances, and see visions, lights, and more. Do not be afraid of them; serve the phenomena and let it teach you what it came to teach or give. Do not get attached to seeing or experiencing phenomena, for in time it will go away. Phenomena experience does not make one who experiences it any more special than someone who doesn't have the experience. If you experience some type of phenomena and you have questions about it, call a minister or spiritual teacher.

A Madonna Moment

As a Black Madonna, the Hindu goddess, Shakti, revealed the play of the universe to me. She unveiled the dance of the paradoxes and the experience that it brings of knowing one's self in the true sense of wholeness. As one is willing to dance between the paradoxes of life, rather than be stuck in being on one side or the other, one receives the gift of peace, of nonjudgmental perception and of self-worthiness.

Most of my life I have been a person who believed that things were either black or white, right or wrong. This kind of thinking kept me in a state of being constantly judgmental and critical of others and myself.

When I came into contact with the Shakti, my beliefs about this thinking began to shift. You see, Shakti is the partner of Shiva and when they dance together, magic happens, for they work together as a pair.

Metaphysically they represent the dance of the both/and. Shakti is the dark mystery of the unknown and the feminine aspect of the Divine. Shiva is the masculine aspect and the known things of life. When they dance together they call forth the highest and best in a person, for they unleash the power of "Cosmic Combustion."

On a personal note:

As I was writing this section on the Dance of the Divine, its sacred movement and ultimate union, interestingly enough my husband and I were invited to attend a benefit dance. The dance was held to raise money for a substance abuse shelter in our area. The theme of the evening and the music was the 1940's swing era.

During one of the sets that the band was playing, a song began to move our souls and we jumped up to dance because we loved the song. The cosmic irony is that we ended up winning a swing dance contest that was being held and we didn't even realize that a dance contest was going on. (The prize was a gift certificate to a fine restaurant in our hometown.)

The song the band played was "Sing, Sing, Sing." We danced because the music touched and moved our souls. As the rhythm of the music drifted across the room, my husband and I danced with a sense of oneness as our movements melded. That was all we were aware of—our oneness and the joy we felt.

The Sacred Work of the Chalice: Meditation Exercises

"I am a Chalice for the Rebirth of the Divine Feminine.
I am a Chalice of Sacred Fire."

1. Chalice Prayer/Meditation: A Body Prayer.

Find a comfortable position, and then begin to focus on your breath. Breathe easily and gently, slowly and consciously. Let your breath take you to that space within where peace resides. Once you feel you have found that place of centeredness, move on to the next step.

Cup your hands together on your lap; place your left hand under your right. Imagine that you are sending down to the cup-like aperture energetic waves of impulses, which represent any problems, issues, or concerns that you are ready to release. Continue to pour your thoughts and feelings into the cup, until you have a sense of completion.

Now, take a deep breath and then move to a standing position, letting your cupped hands rest against your abdomen. Begin to repeat this mantra, ***"I am a Chalice of Sacred Fire."*** Continue repeating these sacred words, but now doing so with a sense of letting go. As you feel the "letting go" move throughout your being, begin to raise your hands and arms outward from your abdomen, then upward. As you raise your arms, let your cupped hands start to slowly come apart. Perform this act of becoming the Chalice with a sense of surrendering, of willingness to release and of being open to the gifts of Spirit (Peace, Love, and Order).

As you continue to repeat, ***"I am a Chalice of Sacred Fire,"*** do so with a sense of releasing and letting go. Know that with each upward movement of your arms and stretching forth of your hands you are opening wider to the in-pouring of the gifts of Spirit.

Raise your arms until they are in a V shape above your head. When you reach this point, imagine that you are a Chalice of Living Energy. The small cup has now been transformed to a magnificent living Chalice. The energy of the Universe is freely flowing through you. Feel this sacred energy moving through the cells of your body. You are a Chalice of sacred energy empowered to go forth and do great things.

Repeat to yourself, ***"I am a Chalice of Sacred Fire."*** (Optional addition to this affirmation: ***"The equalizing, harmonizing, healing power of the Holy Spirit is established in me, now. I consciously release all negative thoughts and live the Truth that I am.")*** All problems live in the human arena. You have now released these issues to the universal fires and have opened yourself to be a channel for the gifts of Spirit to flow through. Accept the gifts in the form of spiritual energy and then from this space of lifted consciousness, dedicate this sacred energy now moving through you to service in the world. Know that the energy of Spirit goes ahead to prepare your way and from It all your blessings flow. Spirit guides your every step. You know what to do and how to serve.

"I am a Chalice of Sacred Fire" is now established within your body. As you lower your arms slowly, sing a song of praise (e.g., Alleluia, Amazing Grace).

2. Chalice Prayer/Meditation: "Whom Does the Chalice Serve?"

Sit quietly. If you are in a group, sit in a circle. Play soft, lovely music. Light a candle. Turn down the lights.Relax your body, close your eyes, and begin to breathe consciously. Breathe in and breathe out slowly and rhythmically. Envision an opening at the top or crown of your head. Imagine that a shower of light, of truth, and love is flowing down to this crown area. Gently, like a spring rain, this shower of light-beads flows through your being, melding to your skin, then the muscle, into the bones, penetrating your organs and tissues and finally down to the cellular level. It permeates every cell and then flows out through your feet. You are now connected at both ends. You are a transformer of energy. The sacred energy you take in flows out to the Earth, the material world, to bless it!

Visualize in front of you, in the center of the circle, a jeweled Chalice of Light. The jeweled Chalice is gold and silver. Gold is for enlightenment and represents masculine energy. The silver is feminine energy and is love. The jewels on the Chalice are the same color as the Chakras in your energy system. At the root is the red ruby, then up to orange citrine, lemon yellow quartz, emerald green, light blue topaz, indigo sapphire blue, and finally at the crown, purple amethyst. Hold this space for a while. Visualize and feel the colors of the Chalice in each of the locations in your body that are unique to them. Do this slowly. Once you have all the "jewels" in place, imprint the entire Chalice into your body and with your next breath, merge with it.

Now ask the question of the Grail quest, ***"Whom does the Chalice serve?"*** Over and over, very slowly and gently, silently ask the question. Keep your attention focused on the entire Chalice; its energy is pulsating within you.

Through the emerald green space of the heart center, feel the bowl of the Chalice filled with the light of whatever you need as nourishment—Peace, Joy, Strength, and Love. Energy is transformed in the heart through love. Now see your heart's desire flowing out through the stem as your sacred purpose in the world of manifestation. See it as God-energy moving through you.

The Body as a Living Chalice

The more I delved into the ways of the archetypal feminine, the more She opened Her heart and ways to me, sharing Her gifts and secrets. The Divine Mother, in Her myriad of disguises and various forms, gave me life lessons that I shall never forget, for She came to share Her wisdom with me.

Many of these archetypal goddesses are known as "Black Madonnas," because they represent the hidden and mysterious side of life and are related to the *nigredo* or blackening state of death in the alchemical transformation process. Black Madonnas are the archetypal guardians of healing through transformation and change and are often portrayed dressed in regal splendor. This royal splendor or queenly image is an archetypal representation of the powerful feminine.

They answered as I called on them for help and gave me ideas for living my life more fully. Each one shared her gifts and her love; and through her generosity, I found wholeness. I danced the dances of life, death, and rebirth. I embraced my shadow aspects and transformed my resistance through grace. I moved frantically and then sat still. I was in awe, fully immersed in their presence, eagerly awaiting their counsel and direction. It was through these experiences that this book was birthed.

As you work with each of the seven Chalices in this next section, you will see that each Chalice has an exercise or meditation and an affirmation for you to use. These are designed to help you incorporate the energy of the Black Madonna, assigned to each Chalice into your heart, mind and body. Consciously, working with these exercises, meditations, and affirmations will help create the solid spiritual foundation needed for initial and advanced awakenings.

Chalice 1—The Sacred Energy Is Within.

Black Madonna/Goddess: Kali.

Her Gift: Destroying vices and giving a sense of fearlessness.

Chalice Location: The First or Root Chalice is at the base of the spine.

Power: Renunciation/Elimination—Expels error thought from the mind and body.

Esoteric Wisdom: Center of generative, creative energy; color, red.

Her Counsel: "It is better to allow the Mystery of Life to intoxicate you, than outside sources."

Invocation: "In facing my weaknesses, I find my true strength." "Out of the appearance of death and destruction arises new life."

Kali is the sacred guardian of the first Chalice. You will often see Kali portrayed as dancing feverishly, wielding a knife in her hand, with her large black tongue protruding from her mouth. Described as being intoxicated with the mystery of life, She dances, destroying whatever is in her path. But her destruction is not bad or evil, because out of death comes new life and Kali knows this. This is her secret power—life, death, and rebirth.

She is very scary looking to the uninitiated for She wears a necklace of skulls. However, if we look beyond appearance to whom and what Kali energy truly represents, we find that Kali is the remover of vices. The skulls She proudly displays are in reality the slaughtered addictions of the human ego. Each of these heads on her necklace represents a negative habit or false belief from which She has "lovingly" rid her patron, e.g., jealousy, greed, aggressive behaviors, lust, anger, She is the shocking force of awakening to a new sense of who we are and to the realization of the splendor of knowing that "I am life and death, dancing."

This Chalice is believed to be the seat of the sacred energy force. It is referred to in the Eastern traditions as the home of the "Kundalini" or sacred energy. This energy lies coiled at the base of the spine waiting the time of its awakening. It is through the rising of this energy throughout all seven of the Chalices that we finally achieve a deeper understanding of what Sacred Union means.

This first Chalice also holds the energy of the thoughts, memories, and beliefs that our family taught us regarding who they were as a member of this group. The family's mind set and beliefs taught us how we would define ourselves within the context of society.

Your family may have taught you that you were a victim of life. But the ultimate choice is yours as to whether you remain locked to that belief system. If you believe that you have the power to create your own reality, then you cannot stand being a victim any longer. If you have the ability to create your own reality, then life is not done <u>to</u> you, it is created <u>through</u> you and <u>by</u> you.

In order to change, you must ask yourself frank questions, such as what is my payoff for staying a victim? Do I like to have people feel sorry for me? Do I elicit sympathy from acting the way I do? Remember, you must be totally honest in answering these questions if you desire truly to change.

If you desire to make changes in what you believe about yourself, to stop defining yourself by who your family says you are or were, then call on Kali. Do not be afraid to enter the luminous darkness where you will find in the deep recesses of your being hidden beliefs, thoughts, and emotions that have defined who you are. From here, you can face them straight on and you can begin to shift your life. Kali energy will help to destroy the illusion of who you think you are and birth you to the splendor of who you truly are.

<u>A Madonna Moment</u>

A Kali Story

The first Dark Madonna/Goddess that I remember having conscious contact with was Kali. We met through a picture. If you have not ever seen Kali, she is an awesome figure to behold. The power She exudes just in her stature is daunting to say the least. In the first image I saw, she had twelve severed heads linked in a chain around her neck, a big black knife-like tongue protruding from her mouth, a carving-type apparatus was in her left hand, and there was a thirteenth head on a platter that she held in her right hand. What a sight! She frightened me horribly and yet, there was something about her that moved me at my depths. I instantly felt as if I were in a love/hate relationship with her.

Kali is an ancient feminine Hindu deity who is thought be about 3,500 years old. Her demeanor and image is enough to make anyone want to back off quickly. It has been said that Kali began as Parvati and was married to Shiva, the Great God of the Dance, who energized the cosmos. Shiva asked Parvati to dance the cosmic dance with him and she agreed. They began to sway and move, slowly at first, then Parvati started to speed up, going faster and faster, dancing more wildly with each step. As her movement became more frenzied and frenetic, Parvati turned to Kali, Mother of Death, and the destroyer.

However, that which Kali destroys is nothing more that our human vices. Those aspects of personality that we hold so dear or ways of being in life that we think protect us from others and from our self. She rids us of vices such as greed, envy, laziness, success at any price, excessive anger, the desire to control, and manipulate. She rids us of them through the power of her "chaotic dance," which reveals itself to us as a discordant experience in our life, an experience that forces us to face every aspect of who we are, positive and negative. Once we are willing to dance with her, Kali becomes not someone to fear, but a source of solace.

Kali subtly reveals this attitude of comfort if you look closely at the nuances contained within her body posture. In all pictures of Kali that I have seen, regardless of how she is depicted or animated, Kali stands with one hand in the traditional position of blessing, which is the universal message that behind every dark cloud there is a silver lining, so hold tight, be willing to walk through this, and there will be a gift for you to receive.

Even knowing all this, something within me wanted to know more about her, even though I knew that I was afraid of the power that she held as the Destroyer of Vices. Often I thought as I was learning more about Kali, "What will she ask of me if I give her full reign in my life?"

And believe me, she did ask plenty of me once I let her into my life! She forced me to look at aspects of my personality that I had cleverly camouflaged for years and years and she asked me to be authentic.

Interestingly enough, shortly after Kali came to my life, I met a man who had lived for twelve years in an ashram in India with Swami Muktananda, leader of the Siddha Yoga linage. It was one of those divine appointments and we soon became dear friends. From the beginning of our friendship, he told me that I carried a Kali-like energy. I wasn't flattered!

I asked him what he meant by that. He said that when he was with me he could be sure that I would trigger some thought or feeling in him that would force him to look closely at himself. Some behavior, feeling, or thought would come to his awareness about himself that, once recognized, he realized he needed to shift or change. Every time he said this, I laughed but something inside me also quivered.

Kali is known as the Destroyer of Vices. Did I really want her in my life and did I want to carry that energy? However, I knew that often when I was counseling or teaching it would feel as if a sacred energy would move in. When this movement occurred, something awesome would (and still does) happen in the room; people would have experiences. They would begin to cry, feel a shift of energy within themselves, or I, by my demeanor, would trigger a feeling in them that they did not understand.

Now, it is a year later. Unrelated to anything we have just previously discussed, I made a decision to purchase a fax machine. I called the telephone company and asked them to give me a choice of numbers for the fax machine. The operator gave me five numbers to choose from; I jotted them all down. When I looked at the list, one suffix seemed to jump off the page, that number was 5254. This number resonated within me; it sent energy throughout my system. I felt it! I knew it was mine! I told the operator to give that number to me.

Three months later I was presenting a seminar out of town. I needed to fax an important bit of information to my husband. Standing in front of the fax machine I started to dial my personal fax number. As I touched the finger pad and as my fingertips slid over the numbers, for the very first time, I noticed the letters assigned to each number.

I gasped as the letters jumped off the machine to my awareness—5254 spelled—***KALI***. My hands began to shake and my body quivered. Suddenly I was aware that she really was a part of life and that she was here to stay and to share her gifts with me.

Over time I became cognizant of the fact that it was a gift to work with and to carry Kali energy. She is a transformer of vices; therefore, she will not let you hide behind facades of self-imposed fear and denial. She works diligently to shift and change the false perceptions and beliefs that have held us back from revealing the full Essence of who we truly are. I knew that I was not to be afraid of Kali or that which she stood for. I slowly came to understand that she would use her energy to transform me and I in turn would be blessed.

If you are aware that there is something in your personality, behaviors, or attitudes that needs to be tempered, changed, or shifted, call on Kali—and get ready.

Exercise/s

1. Grounding through the Ancient Technique of Alchemical Breathing

All of the exercises and meditations in this book are designed to help in the process of conscious personal transformation. As a preparation for each exercise or meditation I would invite you to use this ancient Alchemical breathing technique. The reasons that I have for suggesting that you use this breathing technique prior to each exercise are two-fold: 1. Alchemical breathing is a technique that has been used for several millennia. 2. As you do the work of personal transformation, you are working with the energy field that surrounds you. This breathing exercise helps set the intention for conscious, positive transformation.

In *Breakthrough Intuition*, Rosemary Ellen Guiley shares information about this ancient process of alchemical breathing. In describing the breath work, she confirms that this breathing technique is a simple and powerful tool that carries a potent intention. That intention is to create a circuit of sacred energy that surrounds the body and consciously stimulates the Chalices to prepare them for the transformative work that is about to be initiated.

The two major Chalices that you will be working with during this experience are the root Chalice, at the base of the spine and the sixth Chalice at the third eye. The intention of this technique, as stated previously, is to kindle and inspire these two Chalices to action. Let us for a moment visualize what happens as we participate in this exercise. Picture in your mind's eye a circuit of energy that surrounds your body; this energetic circuit is moving in a clockwise motion around your body from the top of your thighs to the top of your head—moving in a circular fashion around the front and the back of your body. This circle of energy is what you will be creating through the use of your breath.

The Process

The practice is a simple round of breathing that pushes the breath in circular fashion around the outside of the body. You will breathe to a count of four, a number that in esoteric belief is the number of a solid foundation.

Using a count of four for each round, you will breathe in—hold—breathe out—hold—then continue this breathing circuit (to the count of four) in a slow, rhythmic pattern for nine rounds.

To reiterate, one round is considered the following: Breathe in to the count of four (1—2—3—4), hold the breath for a count of four (1—2—3—4), breathe out to the count of four (1—2—3—4), then hold again to the count of four (1—2—3—4). Then the breathing round starts all over again. You will do this nine times.

To begin, stand with your feet planted firmly on the ground and consciously hold your spine straight, with your shoulders back. Bring your awareness to the root Chalice at the base of the spine in the area of your genitalia. Holding your awareness in the center of your body at the base of the spine, begin with your first count of four by inhaling and consciously pulling that breath out from the base of the spine through your lower abdomen. You are taking the breath and consciously pulling it upward toward the forehead in the area of the third eye. Pull the breath to the third eye, and then hold it in the middle of the head to the count of four. Breath out, exhaling through the back of the head, consciously push the air down the spine to the area at the base of the spine. Hold for the count of four here, then begin again until you have completed the full nine rounds.

Once you get the rhythm of this breathing exercise, it is very simple and has the potential to be very powerful.

2. Taking a Stand

Chalice 1 is our connection to our roots and to Mother Earth. By breathing deeply and focusing on the energy in the center of the Earth, we can draw Her sacred energy up through our feet; feel Her power. This is Her way of grounding us to Her; of letting us know that Earth is where we live, not out in the ethers somewhere.

I would invite you to find yourself a patch of ground, a place where you can take off your shoes, breathe, and begin to connect. Plant your feet firmly to the ground and as you do, become aware of your posture. How are you standing?

Do you stand with a sense of firmness, with a stature that says, look, I am a person who knows who I am? Now, take this thought a little further. How do you stand in life? Do you take the steps of life with a lot of soul, or do you tiptoe around trying not to disturb anyone or make any waves?

3. Consciously Moving the Awareness From the Head into the Heart

Purpose: This is an incredibly powerful meditation, which I have used for decades in the "heart awakening" process of transformation. The intention of the meditation is to move our awareness from the head to the heart through conscious intention and use of the Great Golden Light.

Kinesthetic Anchoring — as you participate in this meditation, during those moments when you feel a surge or movement of energy within the body, anchor that energetic feeling, as a conscious memory into the body by creating a muhdra.

How to Create a Muhdra — during the meditation, if you feel a flash or burst of energy anywhere within the body, (using any of your fingers) bring two of them together and create a circle (e.g. thumb and forefinger are brought together to create a small circle, a field of energy). As you bring the fingers together, consciously send the feeling through the heart and down into the fingers to imbue the feeling into cellular memory patterns held within the energetic structure field of hand. Later, when you go into meditation again, use the muhdra to elicit the energy and feeling from the memory patterns.

During this meditation, we will consciously call forth the Great Golden Light from the space of infinity, and invite it to move down into and through the Crown Chalice area at the top of the head. The Crown Chalice is a powerful energy center. When ideas come to us, they ruminate and cogitate in this vicinity, as they gather thought-energy. In addition, this region is home to the intellect, will, reasoning, faith, imagination, and understanding.

Our intention is to have the grand, dynamic, organic, vast, powerful field of golden energetic Light, move through the Crown Chalice and come to rest within the Heart Chalice/ heart-space. This experience is not new; it was practiced during the times of the ancient mystery schools as a part of the preparation work in awakening the Heart Chalice. It is considered to be one of the first steps in the purification process.

If it is possible and you desire to, do this exercise outside. Begin it by standing with your feet planted on the moist mound of Mother Earth, with Father Sky's blue umbrella above your head. Or, begin with your feet planted firmly on the ground, and then lie down on Mother Earth. If being outside is not an option, find a quiet place with a comfortable chair.

Head to Heart – Golden Light Meditation:

Close your eyes and begin to listen to all the sounds that surround you. Become one with your environment, relaxing more with each breath.

Looking through your mind's inner eye (your outer eyes are closed), imagine that a great brilliant, golden Light is moving downward, from a place within infinity, towards the top of your head. As you observe this luminous, dazzling, radiant, golden Light it is apparent that as it is coming towards you and it grows larger and more powerful with each pulsation. In addition, you see that this light is not something separate from you but is actually tethered to you by a golden chord.

As the Light makes it way to the region of your Crown Chalice, at the top of your head, the moment it touches your head, the golden Light penetrates easily through your crown. As the Light penetrates the top of your head, you realize that all of your ideas come to you in the form of an energetic Light.

As the brilliant, golden Light enters your Crown Chalice, you are aware that you can feel the sensation of its energy penetrating the top of your head. Golden Light swirls and whirls throughout the Crown Chakra, until it permeates every cell within your cranium. Dancing Golden Energy infuses your pineal and pituitary glands and then saturates your forehead, and third eye area. Slowly, the pulsating, vibrating frequency makes it way to the back of your head; known by the ancients as the place of entrance for the Sacred Breath. Once permeation is complete, the organic nature of the Golden Light moves itself downward. Continue to be aware of the sensations that you are feeling and where your attention is focused. If your mind wanders, gently return your focus to the specific area that the energy is undulating through, at the moment.

As the Energy of the Golden Light dances its descent into a new area, it creates a shaft of Light that resembles an elevator. This shaft of Light moves past your mouth, down into your throat area; your verbal power and authority Chalice. With each pulsation, golden Energy is shared with every cell it touches.

The Throat Chalice, sends your verbal and energetic messages into the world. For a moment, silently and consciously, bless your Throat Chalice. Give thanks for its ability to communicate the message of who you truly are, easily and effectively. After completing this silent blessing, watch the Light as it is drawn slowly, by an invisible force, down the energetic elevator into the Heart Chalice and surrounding heart-space.

Allow this dynamic, juicy, golden energy to lovingly saturate the entire area surrounding your heart space. After a few moments, the energy fills every cell of the heart cavity, then moving swiftly and deftly, and without pain, the golden Light penetrates your physical heart.

During this time of sacred penetration you may feel a sensation in your heart space; allow yourself to be with the sensations. Dance with them, do not fear the experience.

With this moment of penetration, you have consciously moved your attention, your awareness, from the head to the heart. If a thought, of any type, comes forth seeking your attention, do not fight it, keep your focus consciously in your heart, and allow the thought to reside within your heart space. Consciously, hold your attention in the heart-space as if the thought is arising from the heart. This is what you want to have happen—to have all your thoughts arise from the center of your heart-space – having been tempered first with the Energy of Love.

Bask in this golden energy for awhile, for a time of Silence anchors this energy into the body. When you are ready, gently open your eyes, keeping your attention and awareness in your heart. Go about your daily activities consciously staying focused with your awareness in your heart. When you get into a conversation, consciously keep your awareness in your heart and watch what happens.

4. The Dance of Kali

Are you ready to surrender to the dance of Kali's destruction of your vices and allow the luminous darkness to call forth your light? Are you ready to begin to ask of your self the deeper questions that will release you from your prison of limitation? If so, then from a place of total honesty, ask yourself the following questions and then listen to your heart-wisdom for an answer. (Ask yourself each question very slowly, for a total of three times. Ask and listen.)

Who am I? What do I believe? How am I living my beliefs? Am I who I say I am and is what I do congruent with my beliefs? What is my pay-off for staying a victim? Do I like to have people feel sorry for me? Do I elicit sympathy from acting the way I do?

Once you begin to consciously choose to step out of the self-imposed box of limitation, there is a vast world waiting to receive you and desiring to help you to call forth your unique splendor, glory, and gifts. Be willing to "die" to the old sense of who you thought you were in order that you might truly "live" and that you might go into the world and proclaim your unique good news. Remember, Kali's energy works in Love and from Love so that you might be in service to the universe, universal service that is shared from a sense of knowing yourself as Divine Love in action and not from a sense of being a guru or master.

Chalice 2—Treading the Primal Spiral

Black Madonna/Goddess: Lilith.

Her Gift: Life, Creativity, Sensuality, and Freedom from Repression.

Chalice Location: The Second Chalice is located in the generative/reproductive/pelvic area.

Power: Life—This Chalice has the power to be the betrayer or the supplier of life's creative energy to the body for it governs the life/creative consciousness in the body and without wise council can cause loss of essential energy.

Esoteric Wisdom: Center for Second Birth, transmutes thoughts to action; color, orange.

Her Counsel: "Selfish pleasure, is always followed by pain."

Invocation: "I am a Chalice of Sacred of Fire." "I am a Chalice of Creative Energy, used for Good in the Universe." "I stand in my own sense of power." "I am one with the One, worthy and equal to all." "I accept and honor my sensual nature, now!"

Lilith, for centuries, was scorned as a bad seed. She is now being resurrected to the fullness of what She truly represents as a dark goddess—power, authority, and sexuality. Her energy will help teach you how to be comfortable with your own sense of power and creativity in the world and how to use it wisely for your highest good. As one of the holders of the light around creativity and sexuality, her lessons will draw you out of your fear concerning who you are as a sensual being and She will teach you to honor your creative energy and know its sacredness.

As this Chalice holds the energy for your thoughts and emotions around creativity, power, competition, sex, and money, inherent in this ideas is what values your family instilled in you about each of them.

You can use your creative power to create a new sense of who you are and how you show up in life or you can live with the competitive fear that someone better than you is always waiting to upstage you.

This Chalice center promotes life and holds the space for your vital essence/energy. Life is the expression of Being which manifests itself as animation, vigor, and activity. It is home to our generative organs and is the seat of sensation. Of all the factors that enter into being, sensation is the subtlest and the most enticing. Life and the power to procreate do not live in mind or body. Life is spiritual and its source is consciousness. Life is the acting principle of the universe. Life acts on substance or energy and is guided by intelligence. Life needs a directive power. Whether that directive power or intelligence is our will or the Will of a Higher Power is our choice to make in every moment.

This Chalice influences our sexual activity and power of regeneration. Inhibiting or blocking the flow of sexual energy that moves through this Chakra will throw your body out of balance and harmony. The energy in this space influences the ovarian health in women and the health of the testes in men. The procreative energy force in this Chalice can be used to enhance all forms of creative activity: personal growth, health, healing, intuition, and intelligence. It can also be used to deplete the life force if it is squandered without right use of judgment.

A Madonna Moment

Sensuality and Sexuality

Lilith is your helpmate regarding issues around sensuality and sexuality. Her talon-like feet will help you hold firm to your new beliefs about who you are as a sexual, sensual being. Her power and sense of her own sexual authority are well known. Call on her energies as many have for centuries and she will help you become comfortable with your body and your sense of sensuality.

According to the dictionary, the word *sensuous* "pertains to the five senses." The senses that we know as the ability to touch, taste, hear, smell, and see. Can you imagine what a dull world it would be if we didn't have our sense perceptions and pleasures? One of the roles of the dark goddesses is to help us awaken and remember who we are as sense and sensual beings without guilt or shame. Being sensual and/or expressing our sensuality sexually is not wrong! It is a sacred part of who we are as human beings. The Grand Design called for the senses, sensuality and sexuality, to be an aspect of our humanness, to be inherent in our makeup. Lilith as the

Feminine nature of humankind in its sexual, sensual aspect is a power to be reckoned with. No wonder some people have become afraid of Her, especially when they don't understand Her.

If sexuality is a part of the grand design and we inherently know how to use our sexuality responsibly, what has happened to create such chaos around sexuality and sensuality? How did sensuality or sexuality come to have such a bad rap?

The answer is not so much **who** did this, as **what** did this. And the **what** has a name—I call it "masculine-dominated thought forms." These masculine-dominated thought forms are not just held exclusively by men but by women too. They are certain masculine qualities, traits, thoughts, and ways of being that have soaked the fabric of our subconscious minds and have now become the norm for society. Thought forms—for example, "Success is about power, sex, money and whoever has the most and the best wins"—are polite ways to "do" control and domination.

We, as a society and a world, have been entrenched in masculine-dominated thought forms and their ways of thinking for centuries. These thought forms have impacted our way of thinking, of living, and of perceiving ourselves as men and women in power, in authority, and as individual sensual beings.

Another important word in dealing with our sensuality is the word *comfortable.* Are you comfortable with who you are as a sensuous being? Or do you have an extreme sense of guilt around your sensuality, and sexuality; guilt which has come from someone instilling in you the "badness" of sex, sensuality and sensuousness? This is a sensual world. Take a walk in nature and watch the birds, the cows, the horses, the bees, the butterflies, and the flowers. You can become overwhelmed sensuously with their fragrances and behaviors, watching them glory in the freedom of pure, unadulterated sensuality. This is who and what we were meant to be; again, not without a sense of morality, but definitely with the sense of being okay with who we are and with our bodies.

We each were given a body, not to deny it, but to uplift it to the glory of sacred beingness, which includes Being sensual and sensuous.

Exercise/s

1. Your Desires

Stop and take a breath. Think about what it is that you desire to create. Visualize the scene in your mind, clearly outlining each aspect of your desire. Once you have it defined, cut out pictures that represent the essence of your desire and paste them on a piece of poster board. Hang the poster board where you can see it every day, several times a day, if possible. With the picture in sight, repeat the invocation three times.

2. Your Sacred Sexuality

Do you have issues around being comfortable in and with your sexuality or do you have concerns about another's choice for lifestyle participation? Whatever gender you were born, sexuality is a gift that comes with being alive. But we must accept the gift. For many, we have been raised with all types of taboos around sex and sexual orientation. We are sexual beings, designed to procreate our species through the sexual act. It was created to be pleasurable. Why then, for goodness' sake, would we think that there is something wrong with that which is designed to be filled with pleasure by the Creator? Could **Divine Intelligence** be wrong?

The reason sex has gotten such a bad rap is that we have forgotten how to be responsible—responsible for our own feelings, not someone else's version of who we should be or how we should act. This is not a treatise on advocating promiscuity—far from it. With freedom **to** comes responsibility **for**. With the freedom to explore who you are as a sexual being comes the responsibility for honoring that same act, honoring yourself and your body. You know where that line is!

On page 18 is a meditation. Record this meditation on a tape recorder, using your voice and having Lilith meet you in the cave. Set as your intention the thought that you will ask Lilith for a gift of wisdom or insight concerning (your) sexuality. See what special gifts She has for you.

Chalice 3—Dynamics of the Sacred Being

Black Madonna/Goddess: Inanna.

Her Gift: The shedding of false concepts; understanding the inner Self.

Chalice Location: The Third Chalice is located in the navel or solar plexus area.

Power/s: Strength and Order—Provides freedom from the burden of material thoughts by placing them in right and proper order.

Esoteric Wisdom: Center for purification of lower energies that are transmuted for use by Higher Self, in service to humankind; color, orange.

Her Counsel: "Everything has origin in thought, but from where do you gather your thoughts?"

Invocation: "As I am willing to die to false concepts of who I am, I rise with a renewed sense of oneness of my True Self." "Shadows are but illusions, I Am Real."

Inanna made the descent to the underworld. The underworld represents our descent to the unconscious, where we find and uncover the shadow aspects of our personality...those parts of us that run our daily lives and that we are usually not aware of...those aspects of our childhood that remain within us long after we have grown up but still have their way with us. An example would be a three year old who got his/her way by playing little manipulative games. "Mommy, my tummy hurts. May I sleep with you?" We could say that manipulation at three is cute, (maybe) but if someone is still using it as a coping device at thirty-three, it's not pretty. Learning about what makes us tick and facing all aspects of our personality allows us to live healthfully in life.

This Chalice holds the energy of self-esteem, emotion, survival intuition, physical outcomes, and fears of abandonment, low self-worth, individual identity vs. group/family identity, and our relationship to power in the external world. Its energy contains the dynamics of the sacred in that we must make our peace with the external world in regard to what we will hold as our own personal religious beliefs.

Will we follow our family's indoctrination or will we follow what our heart tells us is the path of our spiritual choice? (This may or may not be the same as the families). It is important always to remember that the negative thoughts we carry about ourselves, which someone else formulated, are unnecessary burdens. We are free to release them and live to our highest potential at any time.

This Chalice's energy, or lack thereof, influences the adrenal glands, which sit within its space. These glands sit atop the kidneys and serve the purpose of helping us in times of attack. The problem is that we are no longer just being attacked occasionally by tigers. We are continually being bombarded with stress-filled situations from traffic, to work, to family, to our own inner thoughts running rampant. The adrenals have a direct effect on many of our bodily functions; e.g., our heart's rate of speed, the blood's circulation, our muscles, and our emotional responses. Excessive use and abuse of adrenalin due to constant stress produces physical symptoms including nervous disorders, ulcers, and chronic fatigue. Making the choice to reduce stress cannot only directly improve the physical body, it also increases self-esteem. It shows you care about yourself.

A Madonna Moment

Inanna and the Underworld

Inanna went to the underworld, was hanged on a meat hook, and "crucified" for three days. (Does this story sound familiar? And it is much older!) Inanna was then resurrected and returned to the upper-world, a better person for having had the experience. Inanna willingly took the journey to the underworld, the world of the subconscious mind. She was not afraid to go through the experience of "hanging on the meat hook" or being crucified in order that she could find out more of who she was.

> Inanna can give you the courage to know that regardless of what has happened to you, you can resurrect to find a new life and a fresh beginning. Inanna represents the time in life when we are willing to go to the depths of our subconscious minds in order to deepen the process of the inner journey. It is a time when one turns her or his consciousness

inward and goes down to the unconscious, the realm where one comes willingly or unwillingly to explore the "shadow" parts of oneself.

Through the acts of surrendering, the wizened ego is released from its egocentric prison. We can move from our own tangled webs of obsessive fears, negative beliefs, addictive symptoms, and distorted behaviors, taking those rejected aspects of our personalities and lives and resurrecting them to a new level of understanding and awareness.

T. S. Elliot said, "The darkness shall be the light and the stillness the dancing." The radiance that shines through the darkness as one shines the light of truth on the shadow aspects of self is magnetic. It is a reminder that although there are those parts of us that have no memory of feeling safe or being loved, there is always the opportunity to rise above these lower level emotions. Those dark places in consciousness can be transformed through the light of love.

Our journey to the darkness often comes in the form of an illness or tragedy. Yet through the "darkness" we are taught how to transform dark, opaque, inert matter to the flowing energy of the sacred temple in which we dwell. The dark psychologically represents that which is still unknown in consciousness.

The darkness of the Black Madonna is actually a radiant light that shines to the dark places to illuminate the shadows and show that they have no foundation or reality when faced head on. The Black Madonna, whether it is in the form of Inanna or others, awaits our willingness to turn inward for it is from there that she can help. Black is colorful. It is mysterious. It is life, ever changing eternal life. In darkness growth occurs, the seed breaks open to revel its sacred contents to the Earth. In the womb's darkness life begins. The journey to the interior is to the place of darkness where one faces the dark, shadow aspects of little self in order that the Higher Self might be liberated, not from darkness to light but to the eternal play of consciousness with its constant change of scenery forever desiring to help us grow.

Exercise/s

1. Reshaping the "Shadow" (adapted)

Purpose: To evoke and incorporate the energy of the "shadow" self.

Material Required: Bread dough, an oven (preheated according to bread dough directions), flat baking sheets, rolling pin, sunflower seeds, raisins, chocolate chips, nuts, and so forth to add to the bread, and paper and pen. (You may do this exercise alone or in a group).

You will need to be seated at a table or on the floor with a clean mat. You will need a piece of bread dough and access to seeds, nuts, raisins, fruit pieces, While the bread is baking you will want to write about what happened during your meditation in your journal. You will write about what came to you during the meditation in regard to your shadow-stuff. This activity will help to consciously call forth your shadow energy.

Process: In order to become socialized in our culture each of us were "required," at some time or another, to stuff the energy around some of our experiences in life, rather than expressing the truth about how we felt. We chose to "stuff" our emotional energy because we did not trust those who were around us or we learned that it was not safe to express what we were thinking. That which we hid, the emotional residue of the energetic thought forms around our perceptions of the incidences of our lives, is known as our shadow-stuff.

Our shadow-stuff lurks deep in recesses of the subconscious mind. However, today we are choosing—consciously—to go forth and meet our shadow-stuff. Normally, this can be done in several ways, through counseling, self-exploration, meditation, and so forth. In this moment, we are going to invite the fragmented shadow parts of our subconscious mind to come forward through self-exploration and meditation. We are choosing to do this in order that these fragmented parts may come forth and be integrated to conscious awareness and thus be healed. Healing enables us to reestablish our wholeness and our holiness.

Directions: Before you is a piece of bread dough. Bread, metaphysically, means substance and substance is the divine energy that underlies all manifestation. All manifestation is a form of energy, including the thoughts that we hold in mind, whether they are conscious or unconscious. Our purpose is to consciously reshape our thought energy.

Prior to working with the bread, you will participate in a brief time of meditation. Following the meditation you will have the opportunity to shape the bread dough to whatever image or symbol came forth in your meditation to represent an aspect of your shadow. Your symbol can be something specific or it can be an abstract representation. There are also items to add to your bread that will help you in "energetically reshaping" your shadow. Let your hands guide you as you create your symbol and allow whatever is within you and desires to emerge to flow through you. The purpose of this ritual is to help you integrate your shadow energy so you can live more consciously as a whole person. While the bread is baking we will take a few minutes to write about the experience.

Meditation: (Remember, in order to keep yourself in a state of good inner balance and to incorporate the power and energy of your shadow-stuff consciously to your life, you need to ritually acknowledge your shadow-stuff. The subconscious cannot tell the difference between a ritual or symbolic act and an actual one.)

I invite you to close your eyes for a few minutes and let your body relax. When you are relaxed, consciously allow your attention to slide from your head to your heart. When you feel your attention in your heart, ask your heart-wisdom the following questions: "What experience in my life am I ready to heal? What am I ready to work on? What am I ready to work through? I am ready to move forward in knowing the truth about who I am."

Allow your subconscious to call forth what you are ready to work on. Don't negate anything that comes up for you. You may not understand its meaning but your inner self does.

Next, ask your inner wisdom for a symbol that will represent that which you are ready to work through. Allow the image or symbol to come forth, letting your imagination give you your cues. Do not negate anything that comes forth; it may be just what you need to ultimately unlock the door to the mystery of your past experiences.

When you are ready, open your eyes and begin to mold your bread into whatever shape begins to emerge. Let the symbol guide you, feeling the energy and power that begins to surface along with it. [Be sure you have provided enough time in order that all (including you) might be able to work with their symbols and feel relaxed at the same time. Once the bread is in the oven, begin to journal.]

Journaling: What images came to you during meditation? What awareness was present as you began to shape and sculpt your shadow symbol? What feelings were you aware of in your body'? How do you feel after having consciously activated some of your shadow stuff? Ask yourself what you can do on a daily basis to privately honor your shadow rather than hiding it or acting it out unconsciously. Continue journaling for ten to twenty minutes or until the bread is baked.

Reshaping the Shadow-Stuff

Once your bread is baked, take your bread and hold it in your hands. Recognize that you have honored your shadow in some way. This is only a portion of your shadow-self that is represented here, not your entire shadow-self. Each day, you are given an allotment of food to sustain you; you are given "your daily bread." You cannot eat today all you will need forever. The same is true of the shadow. You cannot absorb all you need to integrate the shadow in one day. And yet each day you can symbolically eat a portion of it and integrate it into your life in a conscious way. Now, take and eat of your daily portion of your shadow in the silence. Do this in a communion-like atmosphere and ceremony.

Are you willing to make a commitment to yourself to regularly honor your shadow aspect and give it expression in a healthful way that can satisfy and maintain your own inner balance? To close this exercise, describe in one word what the experience was like for you, speaking your word out loud or journal your response.

Chalice 4—Aspiring to Higher Realms

Black Madonna/Goddess: Hecate.

Her Gift: Guarding the crossroads of life, transformation, and protection.

Chalice Location: The Fourth Chalice is located in the heart space.

Power/s: Love, tempered with *Wisdom and Judgement*. From right use of judgment,and making wise choices tempered by Love, intuition and quick knowing arises.

Esoteric Wisdom: Center for Balance and Initiation; color, green.

Her Counsel: "With all choices and decisions that you are called to make, pass them first through the wisdom and counsel of these two."

Invocation: "I accept the 'gnosis–cardia,' the wisdom of my heart's message." "I listen to the Voice within me that guides me to greater good." "Love, tempered by wisdom, leads to right choices."

Hecate (Heck'-a-te) is the guardian of the crossroads of life. As we journey through the experiences of life, we often find ourselves at junctures where we must make a decision as to which way we should go. Hecate knows that when we are at a crossroads, we are at a point of deciding whether we will make a change. Her energy is that of transformation and change. Choose to call on her when you are in doubt and don't know which way to turn. She will respond to your call.

One of the greatest decisions we can make is the one to live from the heart. That is why Hecate was chosen as the guardian of this Chalice, not because She represents love, but because her work is to help you descend to the underworld of your thoughts and feelings, a necessary step in the process of individuation. In these travels, we will begin to ask deep questions. We will question the darkness, the mystery, and the pain that are found on the sacred path of the labyrinth of our soul. The questioning actually takes us forward, moves us, and catapults us to new levels of awareness. We learn that we must make conscious choices in every moment of life about how we will show up. Will we live from a spirit of love or hate, jealousy, anger, fear? It is our choice!

This Chalice is located in the center of the chest at the heart space. It is the center or focal point for the merging of the energies of higher and lower Chalice centers of the body. It is where the spiritual dimension of being unites with the physical. Here the world of Spirit and matter (a derivative of the Latin word *mater,* meaning mother) unite.

The fourth, or Heart Chalice is the source of compassion, love, and the power of forgiveness. The deeper love that is found here is the unconditional love of the feminine aspect of the Divine. This Love cannot be known intellectually; it can only be known through gnosis-cardia, the wisdom of the heart. This Love knows us and waits for us to surrender to Its power of transformation. It is different from any kind of love we thought we had known or experienced. It is not the sentimental and sweet feeling we have always labeled as love. When we are in harmony with this love, we recognize Oneness with and appreciation for every level of the manifestation of creation.

Hecate is not only the guardian of the crossroads, but is one of three women in the story of Persephone and Demeter. The three together, Persephone, Demeter, and Hecate represent the triple goddesses of the maiden, mother, and crone. The three in relationship, personify our personal struggle with leaving the conscious mind (the ego's realm of attachments) and entering the realm of the unconscious

Persephone, that aspect of us which is fresh and ready to be changed, is "invited" to the domain of the underworld. Persephone, at first, goes unwillingly to the underworld, but after a while, she begins to make herself comfortable in the new space. Persephone represents the quality in us that can take lemons and make lemonade, meaning that she can change and transform, regardless of what has been.

Demeter, the mother of the upper world (conscious mind) does not want to live without Persephone, her daughter, by her side (a symptom of attachment to things in the outer). Demeter mourns and laments her loss (the ego always tries to seduce us back to our old ways of being). We all have the mother-aspect that doesn't want to change status quo, that wants our thoughts to stay small forever.

Hecate, as we have said, is the dark goddess who rules the Crossroads of Life. Hecate tells Demeter that she will go to the underworld to "save" Persephone. But Hecate, as the Crone and Wise One in us, knows the value of the journey to the underworld (to the unconscious mind). Ultimately Hecate does return Persephone to Demeter and the upper world, however, not before Persephone eats six pomegranate seeds, which means that Persephone will have to return to the underworld six months a year. Hecate knows that this return is important to the continual cycling of life, for once we have learned the lessons of the underworld, we must return to the upper world and put them to use to practice living what we have learned.

And so it is in our lives. If we are to grow, we must enter the luminous darkness, the realm of the underworld, and discover and uncover the secrets that lie within, then put them to use in our lives or they are of no value. Life is a story of birth, life, death, and rebirth, the continual renewal.

It is only when we have opened our hearts that we can begin the journey to wholeness. Metaphysician, Sig Paulson, says, "The longest journey we will ever take is the one from the head to the heart." When we stand at the crossroads of transformation desiring to change our lives, we must journey to the heart for guidance. This is where the Divine stands waiting to guide us to the right decisions for our lives.

"The journey is much easier if you open the heart first."
—Swami Muktananda

A Madonna Moment

A Forgiveness Story

Hecate took me to the crossroads of life and guided me—as to where to go, which path to take, and when to turn. If you are at a crossroads in life, her archetypal energy can help you make decisions about which way to turn.

This ***Madonna Moment*** shares a personal struggle, which culminated in a new "enlightenment," an opening of the heart. It came through after an illuminating experience that I had while I was in the midst of a deep meditation. During my meditation I felt my heart break open and my being was flooded with a brilliant white Light that permeated every cell of my body. I realize now that it was the Light of Love. On Its entrance to my heart, my mother's face came to view and a feeling of Love like I had never experienced before washed over me. All the tension and hard feeling I had held about my mother melted away. I knew instantly that I had been healed of the past and that I was free!

Immediately, I called my mom to ask for her forgiveness, for being such an unkind and unloving daughter. These are the words that she spoke to me: ***"Toni, I love you, I have always loved you. There is nothing to forgive, my darling, we were both doing the best we could with that which life had given us."*** From that moment on she became one of my best friends.

Love Is the Fragrance

Love is the fragrance that is
Shed upon the soul of one
Who has been hurt
And chooses to forgive.
—T. G. B. (adapted)

Chalice 5—Rending the Veils of Illusion

Black Madonna/Goddess: Mary Magdalene.

Her Gift: Power and authority, a sense of owning that you are the power to change.

Chalice Location: The Fifth Chalice is located at the nape of the neck at the throat.

Power: Power—The power of the Word poured consciously on a Chalice Center, baptizes and cleanses that center of all material thought; removing impotent energy and revitalizing with new life.

Esoteric Wisdom: Center for communicating with the world-soul, and thus God; the imparting of knowledge that is unable to be communicated through speech; formed "the word in the air;"[14] color, blue.

Her Counsel: "Awaken and quicken the centers within you through the power of the Word."

Invocation: "I speak and the world listens, for I know the Source of true Power."
"Through the Power of the One, I choose to live, move and have my being."
"Words sown in and through the Power of Spirit will not return to me void."

In 1945 a set of scrolls, which have become known as *The Nag Hammadi Library,* were discovered in a cave in Nag Hammadi, Egypt. These texts or scrolls are also called *The Gnostic Gospels.* These *Gnostic Gospels* are believed to have been written in the first and second centuries C. E. They are also thought (by certain biblical scholars) to be rejected texts or gospels of the Christian Bible. The relevance of these texts is that they portray and cast a more feminine attitude and disposition to the beginnings of early Christianity. One of the ways that this "feminine spirit" is portrayed is through the description the Gnostic writers give of Mary Magdalene's involvement with Jesus' ministry. It is a ministry of service and active participation within the spiritual community that followed the teachings of Jesus Christ. If we compare these newly found *Nag Hammadi* texts with the now established *Christian Testament,* we will see that the above-mentioned ideas (and many other New Thought ideas) are either ignored and/or excluded from the current version of the Bible.

Several recurrent themes are woven throughout *The Gnostic Gospels.* The first is that every person is able to have a direct experience of the Divine. This experience is called "Gnosis." Another is that the feminine nature of the Divine stands in a position of equality to the Masculine nature of the Divine. These concepts are a breath of fresh air when compared to the patriarchal dogma that has been set forth in current Christian religious beliefs. The conscious suppression of the feminine aspect of the Godhead has had a profound effect on the psyche of society over the centuries. Yet it is well documented that anything which is repressed in consciousness will ultimately resurface at another time in order to be looked at and/or healed.

It would appear that the time for healing of our suppressed feminine is now and it is happening through the assistance of the archetype of the Black Madonna and goddesses. The Black Madonna is resurfacing to conscious awareness through dreams and other activities, such as the archeological findings mentioned previously. Magnetism is being generated through these discoveries that is drawing those "in one accord" to be inspired to look deeper within themselves to find the Truth of their Being from a more deeply spiritual context.

This Black Madonna is not the virginal archetype of Mother Mary. No! This Black Madonna reflects a true woman, one who has "birthed" a child (or a great idea) and is fertile, expressive, uninhibited, sensual, and free to experience herself and life. She is a sacred container in her own right, as She is a "holder of wisdom," which is shared with us in Solomon's "Song of Songs," when She says, "*I am black and I am beautiful.*" "*I am black.* (I am the rich darkness of hidden wisdom being brought forth to the light of the world.) *And I am beautiful.* (I recognize my worth and value as a human and sacred being. I accept the sacred mission which is mine to carry forth to the world.)

Black is a color of growth, of darkness, of creativity, and of wisdom. It is in the darkness of the "womb" where the child and the seed both grow. And it is in the darkness of the unconscious where we too begin find our true Self and grow to the fullness of our spiritual nature. It is time to begin to heal, as individuals and as a collective society, to bring back the forgotten part of who we are: the feminine nature of the Divine. I personally believe that a universal call for the global healing of the "collective" consciousness around the issue of the repression of the feminine nature of the Divine is the major "energetic" force behind the rediscovery of the Black Madonna and the ministry of Mary Magdalene. Her ministry is shared not only in the *Nag Hammadi Texts*, but also in the legends that live in the south of France.

As a woman in the Judaic culture of the first century, Mary Magdalene held this archetype of the black goddess in her consciousness. She knew who She was and was willing to take a stand for what She believed. She was unafraid, thus She was empowered from within through the willingness to change and transform her life. How did She find this true source of power?

In Luke 8:1–2, we are told that Jesus went from city to city preaching, teaching, and healing. With him was an entourage that included his disciples and several women. Luke gives us this description, "And the twelve were with him, and also some women who had been healed of evil spirits and infirmities: Mary called Magdalene, from who seven demons had gone out."

Mary chose several things for her life: 1. Mary Magdalene chose to be healed; 2. Mary Magdalene chose to spend her time sitting at the feet of Jesus and learning; 3. Mary Magdalene chose to apply the teachings of Jesus to her everyday life and thus be transformed in mind, body, and spirit. Mary Magdalene's power came from choosing what was important to her in every moment and then following through with her choices.

What do we really know about Mary Magdalene's life? Very little, other than what has been previously described. But we do know She was a powerful and spiritual person loved by Jesus. And with the release and wide-spread dissemination of the relatively newly found Nag Hammadi texts, we are learning more about her and the powerful role She played in the founding of Christianity.

Mary Magdalene represents the Chalice of Power—and it is one's throat that is its power center. It is the place from which one receives the power of the universe, one's eternal breath. It is the place in one's body from which one speaks his/her truth. The question is, do we? The ability to say what we mean and mean what we say is difficult. Organizing our new thoughts to intelligible words is not always easy, either. From this power center, we have the ability to articulate our needs, describe our feelings, and ask questions, demand answers, formulate abstract concepts to concrete verbiage, and do it with grace and power.

It is from this place that people get a sense of who they are. This is the Chalice from which we communicate our power or lack thereof. Learn to work with this Chalice and to receive the gifts it has to bestow.

A Madonna Moment

An Ode to the Beloved

Mary Magdalene felt the hot searing gaze of His eyes fall on her face.
Pulled like magnet toward iron-filings,
She found herself looking into the eyes of Love.
In that sacred moment Love opened her heart,
And forgiveness washed over her soul.
Whatever she had done, whatever she had been, were now erased
And only the sweet perfume of Love lingered in her heart.
I too desire to have that same Love experience, Holy Spirit.
Pour the Love-substance of Your alabaster jar into my heart,
That I might know, as Mary Magdalene did,
That Love and I are One.
—T.G.B.

Exercise/s

1. Honoring Your Voice

Chalice 4 is your Power center: it is the place where you send thought vibrations to the world through the power of your spoken words. Right now, be willing to get air moving through this Chalice. Sing or chant, to the best of your ability. To begin, try singing a song that is easy to sing, perhaps one like "Amazing Grace." Recall the tune of the song, then I invite you to shift from the traditional words of the song and sing instead the words, I AM. Therefore, you would be singing to the tune of "Amazing Grace," but using the words, I Am. (e.g., I am, I am, I am, I am .... and so on). Let the sound of the power of the words I Am vibrate throughout your being.

Sound vibration, especially when you are using some type of sacred words, literally goes to the cellular levels of the body and creates a shift in the energy stored there. This type of simple vocal exercise is a great way to work with the transformative process of conscious change.

Do not let someone else's opinion about your voice stop you from expressing your own unique song as loudly as you want. Learn to use this Chalice to powerfully speak your truth, to stand firm in knowing who you are and what you decide you can or cannot do. You are a glorious songbird meant to sing your own song.

2. Unleashing My Inner Splendor

***Purpose:** To unleash my inner splendor. To realize who I am, what I uniquely have to give and how I can give it to the world and to take one small step (or large) now!

*Allow yourself to become still. You can do this by taking several deep breaths, watching your breath as it moves in and out. As you breathe in and out, consciously choose to release and let go of anything that might be on your mind about what you have to do today or should be doing now. Feel yourself relaxing. Once you feel relaxed, move on to the next step.

*Ask your Inner Self/Higher Power/Inner *Wisdom* to reveal to you ten gifts or skills that you have, that you are especially good at doing or performing. They do not have to be "mighty," just let them be things that you believe you are uniquely good at doing (e.g., you might have skills in the area of cleaning, organizing, raising money, networking, loving children, honoring women's issues, seeing things that need to changed, drawing, music, and so on).

*Do not discount any gifts or skills that come to you! Write them down; they are all important.

*When you have finished, look at your list. Find ***one gift or skill*** that particularly sings to your heart, one that you believe you can dedicate to the good and upliftment of the world. Remember, when you are willing to change and to lift up your thoughts, you are adding to the upliftment of the consciousness of the world.

("Ah yes, I am really good at cleaning. I can make things sparkle and shine like no one else." Remember, I said that these do not have to be "mighty" in the eyes of the world. This is about you, your gifts, what you do well, and what you can dedicate to the upliftment of humankind.)

*Take your gift and put an action with it, an action that you will dedicate to the upliftment of the world and to humankind. (One person dedicated her cleaning gift to the good of the world by committing to clean the bus stop every other day for a year. Her dedication was to make the bus stop a sweet place for people to wait for their ride.)

* Now do it! Set a time to begin and begin it. Watch what happens to you, through you!

3. Tools for Unleashing Your Inner Splendor: Seven Affirmations

(Speak these affirmations three times per day for twenty-one days.)

"I Re-create Myself As I Accept My Power And Unleash My Inner Splendor!"

1. ***I choose to ask myself deeper questions and to answer them honestly.*** I ask myself in every moment "Who am I? What do I believe? How am I living those beliefs?"
2. ***I choose to sing my own song.*** I will not settle for being someone else' version of who they think I should be.
3. ***I choose to experience life as exciting and fun and to live it that way!*** I will on occasion get a case of Divine Discontent; but when I am chronically maladjusted and negative, there is something for me to learn about myself.
4. ***I choose to accept unwaveringly that the Splendor is within me.*** I do not need to be overhauled to live a new life—I only need to be willing to change and to say YES to life! "Sometimes one has to travel far in order to find what is near."
5. ***I choose to enjoy my eccentricity and to stop sabotaging my good—now! I respect myself.*** "Respect yourself" are the words of a famous old rock song, and that is what I must do.
6. ***I choose to invite the good of life in and to release the rest—with ease!*** What do I want for my life? In order to get what I want I must be willing to invite it in.
7. ***I choose to take time to remember who I am.*** I take time daily to pray. Prayer encircles me in a powerful field of energy. And always, I consciously choose to live from the wisdom of my heart. On the previous page are affirmations designed to invoke the Presence of the sacred power that lives within you. If these do not suit your needs, create your own affirmations. Affirmations are to be spoken with a sense of conviction, power, and authority and are to be repeated a minimum of three times per day, for twenty-one days. This is believed to be the time frame it takes to imprint an affirmation on the subconscious mind.

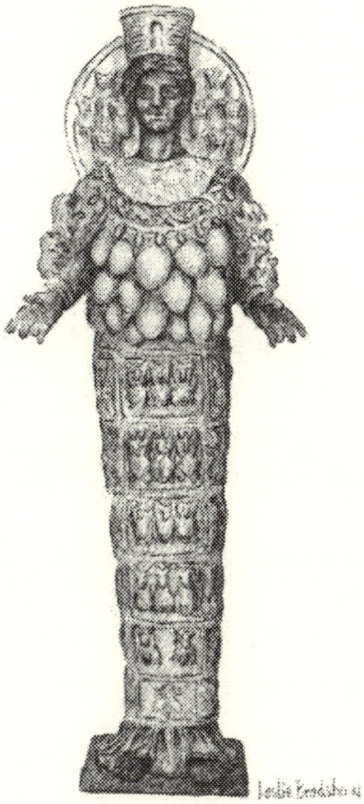

Chalice 6—Emanating the Radiance of Wisdom in Action

Black Madonna/Goddess: Artemis/Diana.

Her Gift: Straight aim, Focus, Wholeness, "One-In-Herself," Strength and Courage to try new things, Discriminating thought, Concentration, New Perceptions.

Chalice Location: The Sixth Chalice is located in the middle of the forehead; also, known as the third-eye area.

Power/s: Imagination, Understanding and Will—In some circles it is taught that the Power of Imagination works in tandem with Faith, however, for this venture we are going to move outside of conventional metaphysical thought and venture forth with a new idea that reveals the connection between, Imagination, Understanding and Will.

Esoteric Wisdom: Center for Life-Enhancing, Radiant Energy; fills speech with vitalized energy; color, indigo

Her Counsel: "Life is an ever-evolving, upward movement of consciousness. Align all the powers, in this third-eye area of the 'Promised Land' through words of Truth, then stand in stillness and behold what appears."

Her Invocation: "I hold words, thoughts and images of Truth in my mind and Universal energy follows those thoughts; moving them to right and perfect completion, according to the Law." "Reveal that which needs to be revealed and heal that which needs to be healed."

Imagination has its center of action in the space directly between the eyes—this area is also known as the third eye—and extends back through the front of the brain and is connected to the brain's imaging or picture making function, near the optic nerve. In addition to this connection, it is purported that Imagination's focusing or imaging power is connected directly to the soul, thus allowing for the ability to project an image to existence through the powers of Will and Understanding (in addition to the powers of Faith, Love, Order, and Zeal).

Understanding and Will, also, occupy an area near the front brain. This front of the brain area has been called the "promised land." These two, along with imagination, rightly understood hold the authority to co-create with you a heaven—or, a hell if abused.

This Chalice center is also known as the third eye; the Chalice of spiritual perception. Through the awakening of this Chalice you begin to connect with the *Wisdom* of the Universe, the clairaudience and clairvoyance (clear hearing and clear seeing). The clear light of wisdom shines forth from here and you begin to know. Your senses are keener and more alert. When this Chalice connects with the heart, you are lifted to new levels of perception and heightened awareness. However, until you are willing to take charge of your thoughts, you cannot expect this Chalice to function fully. You cannot hold thoughts of fear, anxiety, worry, hate, and expect to drink of the fruits of this Chalice.

Diana/Artemis is known to be a stern taskmaster. She does not let you off the hook easily. So it is with your thoughts. If you are going to change and grow, you must be willing to take straight aim with your thoughts. The Law of Mind Action states, "Thoughts held in mind produce in the outer after their kind." Every time something happens in your life, there is a common denominator present—YOU!

But you say, "I didn't want that to happen." Artemis says, "No, maybe you didn't, but you did participate through the thoughts you held on a conscious or unconscious level." She assures you that this is not about blame, shame, or heaping guilt, but it is about finding out who you are at the deepest level of your being and shedding those old beliefs that no longer serve.

You are the root *cause* of your experiences. Your experiences are the *effect*, whether you see it or not. Repeat to yourself, "I am the root cause of my experiences," realizing this is an important step. Artemis reminds us that we must take responsibility and become the straight arrow, using our powers of concentration to take a higher aim when we have missed the mark of higher thought.

(Diana, another name and form of Artemis, is always depicted as being multi-breasted. Remember this when you are in your Artemis experience, for as Artemis/Diana reminds us to take responsibility, Diana with her many breasts, reminds us to nurture ourselves.)

You are a responsible person who has the power to shift and shape the conditions of your life. Blaming others for what they have done to you is an escape route that one commonly uses to avoid responsibility for her thoughts and actions. Even more than this, it is a way that you give away your power! In order to grow in consciousness, you must step away from the monkey chatter or internal dialogue that goes on continually within your mind, saying over and over that someone else is to blame for your predicament. Just as the huntress Artemis must take aim to hit her target, so must you take aim to hit the targets of a success-filled life.

Everyone has a continual internal dialogue going on. Your work is to shift and change this dialogue to be more congruent with your newly discovered state of being. Discovering who you are is not about making yourself guilty for the things you have done in the past, but is about realization—realizing that you have the power to do things differently, if you choose.

When you begin to practice seeing what is truly happening within you and then taking the necessary action in mind to change your course of thoughts, your life will begin to shift. When you take charge of what happens inside your mind, you regain your power. Psychologist, author, and lecturer Dr. Michael Ryce says, ***"Put away your magnifying glass and get out your mirrors."*** This means to stop magnifying the faults of others, being critical of their behaviors, and begin to focus on yourself. How have you participated in what has happened?

You cannot say that you are taking responsibility for life and continue to blame others for what is happening in your life. It cannot and does not work that way! You are responsible for your own responses! "Response-able."

A Madonna Moment

Awakening the Sixth Sense: Intuition

The gifts of include the awakening of the third eye and spiritual intuition. Diana/Artemis knows that self-discovery is the key to awakening intuition and deep skills of inner listening. Self-discovery! That is what this journey called life is all about. Life's experiences are continually urging us to uncover the deeper essence of who we are in order that we might grow in awareness and understanding of the true nature of our being. The question is, "Are we listening?"

The Truths that lead to the revelations and ultimate unearthing of our Higher Self can only be ascertained fully when we are willing to listen to and then rely on our innate inner guidance system—our Intuition.

Intuition. It is a given. Everyone has access to it, male and female alike. Considered as our sixth sense, intuition is a gift that comes from the feminine aspect of Being. The more a person is willing to open to their feminine nature, and in the process trust their intuitive messages, the more "intuitive hits" they will receive. How does one show that they trust these intuitive hits? By being willing to follow through with the guidance that is given to you.

Intuition comes from a place of "mystery" that resides within us. Intuition's mysterious messages often come in forms that we do not fully understand. We may not be able to explain the message or rationalize it from a mental perspective, but we "know" that the guidance given is something that we must do. This "knowing" challenges us to trust, to consciously be willing to lay aside our preconceived notions and reliance on facts, and move forward in faith.

We may go to others for advice, but even then, it is up to us to make the decision as to whether we will follow their suggestions or not. We must turn to our own wisdom for the ultimate determination. Our internal intuitive system is forever trying to make itself known to us, but we tend to shut it out because we do not trust it to lead us in the right direction.

Why is it that we do not inherently trust this intuitive response system? Because over the centuries, intuition has been given a feminine connotation and considered as a "woman thing." It also doesn't appear to be based on facts; therefore, it is perceived as very unreliable. From the intellectual (masculine) perspective, it is only after we have gathered all the rational facts that we can then best determine what to do next. Even though we all have the intuitive capability, very few refer to it as a tool for everyday living. We tend to be skeptical of this faculty and would rather rely on something more tangible—the hard cold facts. Does this mean that if you regularly follow your "intuitive hits" that you would never rely on outer facts or observations? NO! Everything in life is meant to be part of our decision-making process, but the final nudge—the yea or nay—is meant to come from within.

What happens when one engages in this "knowing" approach as a way of living life is that intuition becomes an internal cycle of response. You receive the "spiritual hit," you trust its message, you take action on the guidance that is given and then the process starts all over again. After awhile, more and more intuitive messages seem to come, until finally every aspect of your life has been turned over to this internal intuitive guidance system.

Intuition is often defined as the ability to know the future, but this is not truly what it means. Prophesy is the word that better defines the ability to make future projections. Intuition is about what is happening in the moment and being alert to the "messages" that are desiring to be revealed—messages that can affect your future, but do not necessarily reveal it. Intuition is guidance for the moment.

Charles Fillmore, a New Thought writer of the early twentieth century and co-founder of Unity School of Christianity, states in *The Revealing Word* (on page 108) that *intuition* is, ***"The natural knowing capacity. Inner knowing; the immediate apprehension of...Truth without resort to intellectual means. The wisdom of the heart. It is very much surer in guidance than the head...Through the power of intuition [humankind] has direct access to all knowledge."***

According to modern-day author Dr. Caroline Myss in *Why People Don't Heal and How They Can,* the root of our intuitive ability comes from having a strong sense of self-esteem.

If you think about this concept, it makes sense. When people have low self-esteem, they are more vulnerable to the opinions of others and are usually in a constant quandary as to what to do next. People with low self-esteem doubt that their opinion counts; it takes a sense of knowing who you are and courage to follow through on your intuitive hits, guidance, nudges, and ideas.

"Intuition is not the ability to see the future. Intuition is the ability to recognize the signals that we are being given in the moment. Signals, such as intuitive hits, prodding's, nudges, hunches, a feeling of knowing, a body sensation, an inner feeling, and more. These types of signals inform us that we are to do — something different — than we are normally accustomed to doing. For example, turn left, leave now, call Sue immediately, and don't take that job regardless of how lucrative it seems; the messages are infinite in nature."[15]

Exercise/s

1. Increasing Your Sense of Self Esteem:
"There are no prisons as strong as the ones you create with your mind."

This exercise is designed to help increase your sense of self-esteem, to reveal to you how at certain times throughout your life you have been innately guided and to open you to the in-flow of guidance in the future.

You will need a candle and matches, a pen and writing paper, self-adhesive self-stick notes, a large sheet of butcher block type paper or table covering paper on a roll. The height should be about two feet tall. Cut the length to an eight- to twelve-foot length. Place or tape the paper on your wall.

Write on the bottom of the left hand side of the sheet, the year you were born, and then go forward in five-year increments until you reach the current year. Then go forward five, ten, and twenty-five years to the future.

Review your past, see the moment, and envision your future. It seems simple enough. This exercise, however, is not for the faint of heart or those who are not willing to look themselves straight in the eye and take responsibility for their thoughts and resulting actions. Self-honesty is the prelude to self-discovery. Remember that always. If you want to change, you must become aware of what it is that needs to be or must be transformed.

Where have you been, where are you now, what is your future? What part have you played in the development of the experiences of your life? Where do you see yourself now? Where are you going? These are all questions to which you will find the answers.

Begin by lighting your candle and setting forth your intention for this experience. (It goes without saying—but I will say it—keep the candle away from the paper).

This is a ritual designed to create a sense of your personal historical perspective, to review your life "cycles," to look at "precious" moments within the context of your life as well as the not-so-precious moments and to "see" how you have been innately guided throughout your life.

Instructions

On each sheet of self-stick notes, write one event. Do this according to the best of your remembrance. Write the significant personal events that happened to you over the years since you have been born. Also list the feelings you had that went along with the experience.

For example, 1953—born; 1958—entered school—excited, knew I could hold my own; 1959—other kids started teasing me and I felt ashamed; 1963—feeling as if Mom and Dad never wanted me; 1969—got pregnant—again, felt ashamed, I should have known better, so on and so forth. Make it as personal as possible. If an idea comes to you that would fit under the future, write it up and place it in the projected year.

Another example, 2004 — I am in school but by 2007 I will be out. Mark that event and what you see yourself doing. (This is a free-flowing exercise. Write whatever you want to as you saw it or plan to see it happening, including everything that comes to mind. Do not negate anything!)

Every time an event comes to your mind and you have written it on your self-stick note, including your future forecast, place the self-stick note on the paper on the wall, under the proper year. Once you have finished, stand back and review what you have written. Take time to drink it in. Then take your journal paper and pen, think about the following questions, and write your responses.

Thoughts to Ponder

What do you see objectively (timelines, trends in your life, etc.)?

What feelings emerge as you look at this graph?

What do you see subjectively?

Do you see times where you were guided by something greater than "your mind"?

What questions arise within you as you look at your history?

What obstacles do you see?

Do you see patterns for your life? What are they?

Do you see cycles? What are they? What do you see that you had not thought of before?

How can you use the past history to build a better future?

Where do you see yourself wanting to go?

What kind of action plan would it take to get there?

What elements would you need to make this happen?

Write your response to each of these questions. **Be very honest!** If you see patterns of experiences and feelings that happen over and over, begin to look at them and question their meaning. What can you learn from them?

Chalice 7—The Hidden Mysteries Are Revealed: Wisdom Is Uncovered

Black Madonna/Goddess: Isis.

Her Gift: Resurrection to a new way of life through the restoration and regeneration of that which has been lost.

Chalice Location: The top of the head, the crown area and above—also known as upper chamber.

Power/s: Faith and Zeal—As discussed at Chalice 6, it is often taught that Faith and Imagination, work together to call forth Good, however, we are setting forth a new proposal.

Esoteric Wisdom: Center of the Supreme Guardian of the Secrets. The dual energies meet here to combine, alchemically, to create the radiant light of true purity and illumination; color/s, violet-magenta-white.

Her Counsel: "The dual energies of this area come to union and operate from a center of balance. You now realize the secrets hidden within the depths of paradox and surrender to their Grace." "Look before you leap. Do not allow Zeal to eat up your resources or steal your vitality. Always temper everything you do with counsel from the *Wisdom* of the Heart." "The pursuit of ideas through the intellectual route only, will make people think that you are smart—but where does it take YOU in the end? It is the Energy of the Living Presence established on a base of Faith that builds the 'enduring foundation of character.'"

Her Invocation: "By Grace I live and move and have my being." "I can do all things through the Power of the One that flows through me." "I zealously move forward in the pursuit of Sacred Union." "I have Faith in the power of the Invisible Spirit in me."

Often the faithful are zealots and tend to burn out or impede their growth by running off in all directions. Faith quickens spiritual understanding and thus can be a power for Good in relationship to Zeal and the accomplishment of great things done in the name of Spirit.

In addition, Faith awakens spiritual discernment, which opens our inner eyes and reveals the Truth that lies back of all appearance. So it is Faith that lets us see that there is something Greater to pursue—Union with One—and it is Zeal, "the dynamic power of the great universal impulse that lies back of all action," that provides the "push" to continue our journey until this Sacred Union takes place. Remember however, that Zeal, "the affirmative impulse" of the Universe, must always be tempered with Judgment/*Wisdom.*

Isis, the divine Mother of Ancient Egypt, was believed to have the power to restore life and bring unity to all people. Here is a short synopsis of the importance of her story: Due to jealousy, Isis' husband, her sacred partner and "other half," Osiris was killed by his brother; who then took Osiris' body, separated it, and spread pieces hither and yon. When Isis found out what happened, she knew (Faith) that if she could find the pieces of Osiris' body, she would be able to restore life to him. So standing firmly in her Faith, she moved forward in Zeal—relentlessly searching for the pieces of her "other half." Isis willingly went to the tops of the mountains, then to the depths of seas, in order to find the other half of her being and eventually her search paid off; for she found all of pieces, except for one—the genitalia.

Having found what she believed to be the essential pieces, Isis went to work lovingly reconstructing Osiris and on completion of the task; she stood over him and fanned him back to life with her mighty wings. Osiris was resurrected and the two came together in sacred union to consummate their love. From this sacred merger, a new life was birthed.

This story of Isis teaches us that the pursuit of "our other half," those parts of us that have been submerged, repressed or scattered, due to being torn asunder, is essential in order for the sacred union to take place. We must search for the pieces, regardless of where it takes us, even if it takes us hither and yon, for when we find them—and even if it appears that parts are still missing—we will be restored to new life. We will experience the sacred union and the birth of a new life in the world.

In the sacred nuptial chamber of the upper Chalice, we connect intimately with the Source, the transcendental, the changeless, and the "I Am" of pure being. It is here that the energy of the Earthly realm of consciousness is raised to cosmic oneness and liberation. In this experience of liberation, one senses a bliss and rapture, which is beyond the definition of mere words. The sacredness of these moments of bliss cannot be described when there are no verbal pictures that can be painted to convey to what this feeling of ecstasy is akin.

By drinking in this nectar of the gods, we are filled with an awe that moves us beyond the sense perception of time and space, of hearing and touch. This glorious union is far beyond the grasp of sense and mind. In this place of unity with the Source of Being, there is no I and Thou, there is only THEE! Separation exists no more.

A Madonna Moment

Learning to Fly

The Black Madonna, known as Isis, shared Her secrets of transformation and resurrection with me and taught me how to fly right where I was. She carried me upward, pushed me forward, and gave me strong new wings. Perhaps you have an aspect of your life that needs to be resurrected, perhaps you need a new job, a better relationship, or stable finances. Then Isis is your woman! Allow me to share my story of discovery with you:

As I stated in the Introduction, throughout the early years of my life, I had the feeling that I was like a bird with only one wing. I desired with all my heart to fly, but I was never quite able to figure out how to get off the ground.

Something within me felt incomplete for flight. I lived with the agony of being aware that in the depths of my being a part of me was disconnected, undeveloped, or missing, but I did not know where to find it or how to fix it. I was even unsure what "it" was. The feeling was at times unbearable.

Even after my initial spiritual awakening occurred, I still felt a nagging and gnawing that told me this awakening was only a beginning. I knew that I had not arrived at my spiritual destination; there was more to experience and grow through.

After many years of treading the spiral path of spiritual evolution, "The Black Madonna" (a.k.a., the feminine nature of the Divine, the Cosmic Mother) tiptoed into my life. Silently, from the depths of my being, She made Herself known to me and changed my life forever!

She opened the portals of my mind, heart, and being to new horizons. She challenged me to shift from linear thinking to a more inclusive and abstract way of looking at life. Within the mystery of this transformation, I discovered

The other wing of my being,
the feminine nature of the Divine.

It is from this incredible discovery, of reclaiming the feminine nature of the Divine that I have now been able to stretch forth my wings and truly fly. And, oh, what a flight She and I have shared! We have been to the highest reaches of heaven and to the depths of hell. In each place She has shown me the glory, the mystery, and yes—the agony hidden in their midst. She has stirred within me the desires of a passion for Oneness with the One, a desire that burns greater than two lovers plunged to the heat of ecstatic foreplay.

She has taught me that to know myself as the One is the greatest treasure I could ever hope to attain. In mystical moments with Her, She has taken me by the hand and asked me to meet the unknown aspects of myself in the oddest of places. Together we have traversed mountaintops and soared to the realms of higher spaces.

At other times She has plunged me to the darkest recesses of my hidden inner consciousness. In these dark places I have been burned by the alchemical transforming flame of Her fire, a burning fire, that has often had me begging to be released from its flame and at the same moment knowing that Her fire was all I desired—for I knew within, it was the glory of Oneness with the One (God).

Exercise/s

1. The Guardian of the Chalice

The Chalice, with its energetic liquid overflowing and its upwardly progressive movement throughout your body, awakens you at many levels to the spiritual journey. On the spiritual path you will learn to embrace the luminous darkness; if you lack the courage to go in search of your own "demons" or foibles, your quest for union will fail. It is the lessons that the demons (your inner wounds and human frailties) teach you that will ultimately heal you. Standing firm (remember Chalice 1) in a sense of self-responsibility, releasing your victim status and the "they did it to me" consciousness, can begin to move you forward.

The sacred energy flows upward through the Chalices—letting each lesson of life teach you. Realize that it doesn't matter whether the lessons are bitter or sweet; for it is in facing your wounds and healing that you grow. And it is through this growth to the Truth that you will finally attain Oneness, the goal of the Chalice adventure.

Instructions

You will need a pen and paper; a chalice-type cup; a clean small cloth; an altar; candles; matches; wine; juice or water.

Place your candles, cloth, and Chalice—filled with a few sips of the liquid of your choice—on the altar. Light the candles on your altar as an invitation to the

One to be present with you during this ceremony.

Begin the ceremony with *The Living Chalice Prayer (on next page).*

While reading the prayer, hold your chalice. After you have completed the prayer, be very conscious of the Chalice, feel its weight in your hand. Become aware of its contour; think about what the shape represents to you. Begin to imagine that your Chalice is a symbolic representation of you, as a sacred container of the essence of life.

Ask yourself the following questions:

"What does the chalice represent to me?" "What does the sacred nectar of the chalice represent in my life?" "What are the wounds of my life that the nectar of the chalice has come to heal?" (Name your wounds, be specific, and give them labels. Do not negate anything that comes forth.) And again, "What does the chalice represent to me?"

Set the chalice down, take your pen and paper, and write the thoughts and feelings that come to you about what the chalice represents in your life and the wounds that you have identified?

Now take the cloth and place it over the chalice. As you cover the chalice, imagine that you are placing a covering over your Essence. Pick up the covered chalice and hold it in your hands, ask yourself these questions:

"What am I trying to hide?" "Why do I want to hide my glory?" "Why would I want to cover my greatness?" "What am I afraid of someone seeing?" "How does my playing small serve me or anyone else?" "What have I been holding onto in life that has perhaps been holding me back—holding me back from receiving the best that life has to offer?" "What do I want to continue to hold onto in my life?" "What do I want to let go of?" "Who does the chalice serve?" "Who do I serve, really?" and finally "What is it in life that I want to serve?"

Set the covered Chalice down.

Take your pen and paper and write out the thoughts and feelings that are flowing through you. Just keep writing, let one thought flow to the next. Do not negate any thought or feeling that comes forth. Be willing to observe them!

Take the covered Chalice to your hands. Close your eyes and give thanks for this experience and for your feelings, then slowly take the veil/covering off the Chalice. This is a symbolic representation of the veil being lifted from your eyes. Bless the glory of the Truth of who you really are.

End this sacred time by reading again *The Living Chalice Prayer* that follows.

Now, bless the sacred nectar inside the Chalice as a symbol of the sacred energy that lives within you. Then take and drink!

The Living Chalice Prayer

Infinite Energy, Loving Presence, to Thee I surrender. Surrender
Not as in a giving in, but as in a conscious giving over
Of my egoistic identity to a Power greater than
Myself. I know that it is only when
I am emptied of self, dear Presence, that
The spaciousness is created which
Allows me to be filled with Thee.
Fill me with Thy *Wisdom*, Thy
Peace, Thy Light, Thy Love, and Thy Life.
Teach me of Thy Sacred ways. Reveal to me
In every moment that which is mine to know
And heal me at depth. Full and overflowing, each
Chalice Center within my being takes Thy Sacred
Liquid Light of Spiritual Energy and sends it forth
Throughout my cellular structure and energetic field. United now with You,
The Chalice of my heart offers Your Sacred Nectar to the world. It is with Thy Grace
That I go forth each day to share the glory of Thy Love, Thy *Wisdom*, and Thy Light.

—T.G.B.

EPILOGUE

The Spaciousness of Emptiness: Prove <u>*ME*</u> Now!

***"Prove <u>ME</u> now, says the Lord of Hosts.
See if <u>I</u> will not open the windows of heaven
And pour forth an abundance of blessings."***
—Malachi 3:10

Have you ever been haunted by an unsure or an uneasy feeling, a sense of a "something" unnamed that would not let you go? This is how it has been for me in the completion of this book, for it has taken me years to finish. Every time I thought the book was complete, an interior sense of non-completion would haunt me, and I could not move forward on getting it ready to go to the publishers. Now I know why. For how could I finish something that had as yet, not found its ending? However, it is finished now, for the culminating experience that I am about to share has brought it to completion; and now, I am ready to move forward.

Yet, as I try to put the final words on paper, words that will tie everything together and bring it to closure, "I stammer," for how does one explain in prose a life-altering experience? For help, I turn to the words of Angela Folign, a thirteenth-century mystic. In Folign's "An Experience of Oneness," she too protests that she only "stammers" as she speaks, because no words can convey the magnificence of what she has just experienced. Here is what she shares:

"All this is beyond anything that had happened to me before . . . I truly felt a Divine change take place in my soul, which I could not describe or explain if I were a saint or an angel or any other kind of creature on earth. This change was so profound that [no one] could fully understand it, and this is why it would be blasphemy for me to try."[16]

And now I echo that same sound, "How do I convey the 'music' of the angels in mortal language or symbolism?" If it were not that my heart—along with a few friends—was urging me to share the mysteries that I have personally experienced, I would not do so! I write of my experience because perhaps there is someone else who is in need of reassurance and support. Perhaps there is someone, this very moment being "burned" in the fires of the Divine Mother's love and they do not understand what is happening to them – for them I write these words.

If you are experiencing what appears to be a life-threatening illness, or a dire life-situation, and you are reaching out for words of comfort and hope, it is to you and to this end that I write of my own "burning" experience. To be burned in the fires of Love, and to know that it is Love that is doing the burning is something that many mystics have written about over the centuries; to read about it is one thing; to experience it is another matter.

The Story:

Standing at the threshold of another year, my doctor informed me that it was time for a mammogram. Dragging my feet for a while, I finally made it to the hospital on June 3. The next day, I received a call from the hospital, saying that I needed to have a follow-up test, because the mammogram revealed a place on my breast that looked "very suspicious" and needed further investigation. Three days later, accompanied by my husband, I went back to the hospital for a sonogram.

After reviewing both the mammogram and the sonogram, the radiologist came to share his findings. I gave him my usual retort, "I have a master degree in nursing, so tell me everything." He agreed. Then with the saddest eyes, he looked at me and said that in his opinion what we possibly had was tubular carcinoma—breast cancer.

Interestingly, I felt no fear around the diagnosis; however, immediately I said to my husband, "We will tell no one." As soon as I said those words, I felt a veil come down across my heart.

My reasons for not wanting anyone to know, I can see now, had their foundation in fear. The first reason was that I did not want anyone to look at me the way that doctor did. I needed to stay focused, and pity wasn't going to help me. The second reason, and probably the most important to me at the time, was that I did not want anyone at work to know, because after all, what would they think of me? I could hear them saying, "Toni is a minister, a metaphysician, a mystic, a writer about the deeper issues of life, and there is something "wrong" with her; how could this be?" With the veil of denial anchored in place, I comfortably moved into denial and left the X-ray department, laughing.

Later that same night, a coworker called to complain about a slight she had felt. I couldn't connect with her issue. All I could hear was, "Blah, blah, blah." I wanted to scream, "You think this trivia is important; listen to what happened to me today!" However, I remained silent. I knew she felt that she was not heard—and in that moment I felt I had nothing to give that could make that happen.

The next day my family physician called to advise me that I needed to stop taking the medication that I had been on for years and to stop all caffeine intake. I did as was suggested, and within a few days, between the denial and the withdrawal symptoms, I was, as a friend later described me, "a wild woman in motion."

By the end of the next week, several things happened on the same day that brought to my attention how out of control I was and the depth of the level of denial that I was in. The first thing that happened that day was that I became very angry at a coworker and proceeded to share with her, in a not-so-gentle way, just how angry I was. After it was over, I was sitting in my office thinking about all the reasons why the interaction was a justified one when a thought crossed my mind that said, "Is hurting someone, because you are hurting, worth it?" It jolted me! New thoughts began to roll around in my heart. I heard my little sacred voice asking, "Toni, are you projecting your own anger on someone else?" "Toni, are you in denial?"

Later that afternoon, I went to the doctor's. As I sat and listened to her speak about the "cancer" and what should happen next, I felt as if she was talking to someone behind me. I was not engaged in the conversation and I was conscious of the fact that I was not engaging. She talked on about making an appointment for me to meet with a breast cancer specialist in two weeks, which we did, and then I left. After exiting, I realized that I had not asked her one question. I began to think that that was very strange, that I had not asked her anything? Again, the thought bubbled up, "Toni, are you in denial?"

The last incident of the day occurred at about 8 p.m. I was at home and the same coworker who called the week before, called again. This time she wanted to discuss another work issue that was of importance to her. She was asking me to change something regarding an event that we were both involved in. We stayed on the phone for more than ten minutes. It seemed like an eternity. She was looking for a win-win situation, but every proposal I shared with her, she didn't seem to like. I began to feel like I was using a tremendous amount of energy trying to work on a problem at the level of the problem. Not only that but I felt as if I was at the end of my rope. I felt the pressure mounting, I was ready to explode like Mt. Vesuvius, and so I told her I didn't have any more resolutions to offer and that I had to hang up. Now!

As the phone call ended, I was frustrated with my friend, with the situation, with myself, and with feeling that things were out of my control. I was unhappy that I denied myself the ability to say to my friend, "Look, right now I can't talk to you about this; I am in the midst of a personal crisis, and I need you to pray with me."

Suddenly, I started thinking about the teachings I have been steeped in for the past thirty years. Were not these teachings about seeing life from the greater expanse of Reality and not the limited perspective of the problem? Did I believe that each experience of life comes to bring me a gift, if I am willing to "lift up my eyes," above the level of the problem to the level of Spirit? Is not everyone playing a part in the scenarios of my life; parts that will result in my soul growth, depending on the choices that I am willing to make in any given moment? And if I choose to live from this higher state of awareness, will I not see only Love and the lessons that Love brings forth for me in the moment?

With this remembrance, I thought that perhaps the experiences of the day, including the phone call from my friend, were playing a part in my destiny. Suddenly, a tear slid down my cheek, and the accumulation of the pressure from the events of the week revealed their shallowness—I was not living in Love. Neither was I loving myself, nor anyone else, by keeping everything a secret by denying what was happening in my life.

With this thought, the tear became a river and the river became a flood. I began to sob uncontrollably. The grieving process had begun. I realized that I was not grieving because of the diagnosis, but because of the fear around my precious self-image. Funny, I was not afraid of a diagnosis of cancer; I was afraid of what people might think about me because of the diagnosis.

In an instant, I knew that the fear of what people might think about me was a major part of what this experience had come to teach me. "YES!" I had to Love me—regardless of what others thought about me, I had to be important in my own eyes. I had to release the feeling that this diagnosis was a form of failure on my part. Suddenly, the job and the facade that I wore of being strong, perfect, being there for everyone—none of these mattered anymore—only God and Love mattered.

Who knew about the diagnosis didn't matter anymore. Who I shared the diagnosis with was not a consideration. In fact, the world could know. I didn't care! It didn't define who I was! I didn't know why this experience had come to me, or what it had come to teach me, but God did and that is what is important. I would surrender to a greater Power and walk through whatever was in front of me.

The next morning (Friday at 9 a.m.), I was on the porch of our CEO's house, ringing the doorbell. I shared what was happening with him and his wife, and they both assured me of their total support. How could I have thought that he/they would do any less? I realized that "denial" and the feelings associated with it play funny tricks with one's mind. I was beginning to see how and where denial had taken me over the past week.

As I stated earlier, the tears started flowing on Thursday night, and they lasted for days. In fact, I cried from Thursday night until Sunday afternoon, and I cried like a floodgate had been opened. Sunday was a perfect June afternoon. About 3 p.m., I was sitting on my deck communing with nature and reading a book by my favorite author, Joel Goldsmith. I had just finished drying my eyes after a little spurt of tears when I heard the wind rustle and behind it came a voice which said: "What now? You have denied, and you have cried. What now? What are you going to do now?"

It was as if something had just hit me in the solar plexus. I gasped for air and immediately I knew it was time for me to stand in Faith and to do as Malachi 3:10 suggests, "Prove **Me** now." It was time to put to work the Truth principles that had been brewing within me for the last thirty years. I felt that my breast represented the Mother, matter, love and nurturing on every level—spiritually, mentally, emotionally, and physically—and I knew my lesson was to learn to Love me, to let God-Love be released, from within me on every one of those levels and within every cell of my being.

Instantly, something shifted inside of me. I felt an energy of **hope**, and a sense of assurance surged through my cellular structure. I knew that I was going to go to work the next day and share with everyone that I was taking a leave of absence.

And if I were to return from the leave, I wouldn't return until I was healed, whatever that meant. It was also clear that it did not matter what projects I had on my plate, or who I thought I would be letting down by taking the leave. This was about me, and I mattered!

I was aware that the denial that I had been carrying kept me at the level of the problem, and Spirit was asking me to work from a higher level of awareness. I had no fear now, about anything. I didn't know what was going to happen, but God did and my job was to surrender to Grace of God and to allow the Glory of God to shine forth through me.

The next day I went to work, stated my claim, cleaned up a few things and left. This was a major step for me; I was leaving my identity. I did not know if I was ever returning—and it wasn't important. This was about taking on a new identity, like a federal witness protection program, however, I refer to it as the "Christ Protection Program." (I say this fully knowing that when one is a new creature in Christ, one does not need any protection for there is only One Presence and One Power and in that consciousness there is nothing to protect.) I left work with no regrets and did not look back.

For thirteen years my heart-quest has been one of getting to know the feminine nature of the Divine, at my deepest level. I wanted to understand, embrace, and embody the feminine qualities of God, and perhaps this breast experience was the Holy Mother's (the Holy Spirit's) way of fulfilling my desire.

On reflection, I thought about how I had not learned how to love and nurture from my mom. My mom and I did not have a nurturing, loving mother-daughter relationship. Now, it was time to stop lamenting over what I had not experienced in my childhood and to discover all those attributes that I desired, within myself.

Intellectually, I knew that as Mother-type energy, the feminine embraces the qualities of compassion, love, and forgiveness; holds the space for birth, death, and rebirth; walks with us on our journey into the darkness and the mystery of the unknown; and through Her "burning" experiences strips away our veils of illusion.

Sitting on our deck, which overlooks a lake, I sought solace in this Mother-God energy and I held one intention to understand Her as the Void, the Mystery, the Glory, the Silence, and the Spaciousness of Emptiness. Let me share this, for it is very important. ***Not once during my whole experience did I ever pray for God to heal me.*** When I prayed, I asked only, to have the Glory of God revealed. I knew in my heart that if I could connect with a deeper understanding of the spaciousness of emptiness, I would be touching the place within me where nothing exists and yet, from which, everything is birthed.

From pre-dawn to mid-night or later, each day, I sat on my deck communing with the Mother-God energy, as I understood it to exist. I listened to Her earth sounds, observed Her rhythms, and watched Her creatures as they allowed their intuition to guide their every move. It was a sweet time. One evening I became aware that my thoughts had become so still that I had become entrained with the movement of day to evening. There is a perceptible moment when the bustling of the day shifts into the song of the evening. I realized that the indigenous people knew this and that is why they considered the Earth so sacred and revered Her as the Mother.

I began to see that in every moment my prayers were being answered, and the Glory of God was being revealed to me. Love was being drawn to me from everywhere as I tapped the well of love within my Soul. Drawing from this Source, my world was being made new. The words of Paul from Ephesians "Behold, I am a new creature in Christ," is what I felt. I was standing firmer than ever in my faith that all things are possible through God consciousness. "I, the I AM, in the midst of me is mighty." Not I, Toni. I can't heal myself, but in surrendering moment to moment to a Higher Power, a Greater Will, I was being renewed in mind and body.

During a contemplative moment, I thought to myself, "Imagine what a risk it was to ask God to understand the spaciousness of emptiness; what were you thinking?"

I heard the words, "I am that I AM," as if it were a musical note, resounding throughout my body temple, and I was aware that the Grace of God began to hold me in Its embrace, letting me know that I am Love and I am Loved!

In a flash of inspiration, it became clear that whether or not a physical healing occurred, it really did not matter. My soul was being cleared of the layers of murk and muck that had accumulated over a lifetimes, and this was the REAL healing! I was at Peace and everything was in Divine Order—regardless of outcome. I knew that and meant it, from the core of my being.

Everything that needed to happen around the breast issue took longer than normal. Due to "uncontrollable" circumstances, the visit to the breast surgeon couldn't happen right away; it took an extra two weeks. After I did see her, because I had been taking an aspirin every day, we had to wait seven to ten days longer for the biopsy. When I learned of all these delays, I decided not to get upset, but just to take a deep breath and remind myself that I had asked to understand the spacious of emptiness. These delays provided me the opportunity to sit in the mystery of it, contemplate God as Mystery, and believe me, it was all a mystery to me!

In the meantime, I felt guided to continue in my new routine. Up at 4 a.m., go to the deck, pray, contemplate, read, and listen for the still small Voice until about 9 a.m. At 9 a.m. I went to my neighbor's pool where I did water aerobics with a few women friends. Whether they knew it or not, they were a great source of strength for me during this time (we called ourselves "The Girls of Summer"). After aerobics, I would come home and resume my previous routine until about 12 midnight. Sleep did not seem to be a priority for me as much as sitting on the porch and communing with nature, the stars, and the moon and feeling their energetic pull.

Each night, under those stars, the smallness of all life's issues became clear.

Clarity, focus, insights, and intuitive thoughts became my new friends as I wandered through their terrain—the present moment. The power held within the spaciousness of the present moment was becoming clearer and clearer to me.

On the Sunday before my visit to the breast cancer surgeon, I had my first alternative healing session. A healer, steeped in the study of bioenergetics, came to my home. She had studied for four years at the Snow Lion School for Healing in the south of France. The evening was perfect, the wind was still, the sun's rays had warmed the deck, and I felt like a newborn wrapped in a freshly heated blanket. It felt like the Mother was cuddling me in Her arms and holding me next to Her. The healer said little. She went about setting the space and requested that I lie down on the chaise lounge, close my eyes, relax, and trust that the Spirit within me knew what needed to occur.

We started the treatment about 7:30 p.m.; the last thing I remember was her invoking the energy of her guides and of the "Elders" and asking them to assist her in the work because she was just a vessel for a Higher Authority. I did not regain conscious awareness until about 10:30 p.m. I can only think that this must be what it is like when someone is "slain in the Spirit."

During this period of being "out," I was very aware of the "Elder beings." I could feel an energy moving throughout my cellular structure; it was as if I was receiving a warm, liquid transfusion of Light. The next morning as I was sitting in meditation, I noticed a strange feeling within my breast. It was as if the white blood cells were "chomping" on a meal of residue. The thought made me giggle.

Please know that when I shared my personal experiences with the healer, I was very clear that healing can only come through the Higher Consciousness within oneself. Even Jesus did not heal anyone who could not tap into, or entrain with, the Higher Consciousness that He was holding.

"***YOUR FAITH*** *has made you whole,*" Jesus said to the woman with the issue of the blood. Not His Faith, but hers! Jesus walked through the crowds, and many were not healed because they did not have the Faith. And to the ones that were healed, He said, "Go and sin no more, lest a worst thing befall you." With these words he meant, do not hold negative beliefs or error thoughts anymore—know the Truth about who you are!

Finally, the day arrived; the visit to the breast surgeon. She carried a very Kuan Yin-like energy and I felt safe in her presence. We (my husband Jay and my friend Wendy) reviewed the mammograms and sonograms with the doctor. Dr. J. showed us the "evergreen clumps," the area of the tumor.

Jay and Wendy sat there quietly, holding a space of love and compassion. In an instant the Light of awareness struck me, and I heard the words, "Do you see the power of illusion? 'Judge not by appearance?' What are you going to believe?"

This was my Soul speaking to me and I was being asked what I was going to choose—the content of judging by appearance or the spiritual context of Truth? It was a universal moment in time, the choice could, would determine the rest of my life.

I was clear that it was my Soul speaking to me, and I had to choose. I chose God! "Prove ***ME*** now," I would place my faith in One Presence and One Power, Unchanging, and Eternal. The nature of God is Love and Its function is to maintain, sustain, renew, regenerate, and govern all the beings of heaven and earth. And Its job is to do this work, in not just a partial way, but totally and completely, as It holds everything in an embrace of perfection, balance, harmony, and wholeness. This is the Truth, now and forever.

As was mentioned because I was taking an aspirin a day the biopsy was delayed a week longer. During this time I had another alternative healing session. It was a repeat of the last time, except this time she invoked the presence of the higher realm of angels. As soon as they were invoked, boom, I was out. Again, I did not come to for over two hours, and the sense of their presence with me was strong.

Let me digress here for a moment, for some may question why I was continuing with conventional therapy. My faith was stronger than ever and yet, so was the guidance that I had to follow through with both kinds of therapy. I knew I was to do this until I felt differently about one or the other. It may seem strange, but that was my path and I was clear about the direction I was receiving. I was "being told" in my prayer times that I was not to resist anything that was placed before me as therapy unless Spirit clearly directed me to do differently. At this point, that had not happened.

Finally, the day of the biopsy arrived. The biopsy room at the Breast Cancer Institute was sterile. I was alone in the room since no one was permitted to accompany me on this part of the journey. Jay was in the waiting room. He was not alone because there were many other women in various stages of breast cancer therapy awaiting their specific procedures. I was in the biopsy room lying on a palette-like structure waiting for the radiologist to appear. The breast pictures were once more displayed on the special light fixtures, and I looked at them and thought, "Oh, those are interesting." Then I blessed whatever gift they had come to share with me.

After the radiologist arrived, we went over the pictures and the "evergreen clumps," one more time. Then he set about his work. His actions reminded me of an elf getting ready to pack the Christmas stocking. He said that he would do another sonogram so he would know exactly where to make the needle punctures. As I lay there, I was aware that I was not afraid, regardless of what happened, I was clear that a Greater Power was in charge of my life and the Universe.

Deftly, he moved the probe across my breast tissue—across, up, down, sideways, and every which way. After a short while he looked over at me and said, "My dear, we will not be doing a biopsy today -- there is nothing here -- you are free to go!"

We talked for a few moments; he was not sure what had happened, but he was sure that whatever was on all the various x-rays and pictures was not there now. I left and got dressed. When I walked into the waiting room and saw Jay, I began to cry. He took my hand and said, “Honey, did the biopsy hurt that bad?” In the midst of the tears, I smiled and said, “No, they didn’t do a biopsy. I was healed, everything is gone. It is a miracle!”

It was one of those surrealistic moments of life. Suddenly; all the women in room began to clap. The air was filled for one precious moment with a palpable feeling. I felt it, they felt it, we all felt it—it was electric. It was as if we were caught in a timeless moment, in the space-time continuum, and the energy of all the women, both past and present, came in to join with us in a bond of sisterhood. I say this knowing that perhaps only those who have been to the edge can understand how it felt as we stood together in a moment of HOPE and HEALING for all!

God is Good All The Time,
Yes, She is!

Individual and/or Group Study Questions

(For Group Work—Please journal your thoughts first, then share them with the group as directed by the facilitator.)

- What significance, if any, does the Divine Feminine's return to conscious awareness hold for humankind and the future of the evolution of consciousness?
- What is an archetype? What role/s do archetypes, dreams, and/or symbols play in our lives and in spiritual transformation?
- When we talk about the "shadow-aspects of self," what do we mean? Have you ever confronted your "shadow-self?"
- Have you ever heard of the Black Madonna? How did the Black Madonna make Herself known to you? What gifts, if any, has She shared with you? What gifts has She come to share with humankind?
- If someone asked you about the Divine Feminine or the Black Madonna—who She is and what role does She play in our lives, individually and as a collective whole, —what would you say? What does She, personally, represent in your life, if anything?
- Is God a woman or a man? If God is continually portrayed as masculine in gender, in whose image are women made?
- Who is Sophia of the Bible? When you were a child in Sunday Bible school, did you learn about Sophia? As a prominent figure in early religious history, how was it that Sophia became virtually an unknown character? How or through whose influence was Sophia's role in religion eliminated and/or repressed?
- Are you afraid of the dark? What have you been taught about the dark and darkness? After reading the book, what are your current thoughts about darkness?
- Which of the exercises in the book, if any, did you resonate with? Why? What did it elicit from you or trigger within you?
- Do you see the energy of the Divine Feminine as a catalyst for change in the 21st century? If so, in what way?
- Did you participate in the Chalice Exercises? If yes, did you experience any feeling or release of energy in any area of your body? If yes, where and what did you experience?
- What are your feelings about Mary, the mother of Jesus? Do you see Her playing a significant role in the lives of humankind over the next century? What message/s is She bringing to people as She makes her appearances throughout the world?
- Who are you? What is your story? How do you define or describe yourself in relation to your story? What do you want people to know about you? What are you afraid that people might find out about you?
- Are you afraid of death? Are you afraid of dying (in whatever form it comes)?
- What forms have the Crucifixion experiences of your life taken? What forms have the Resurrection experiences taken?

GLOSSARY

Archetypes: a pattern of energy held within the collective unconscious mind and recognized within our psyche for the pattern of energy, which it represents (e.g., the hero). Other archetypes that might be familiar to you are those of the wicked stepmother, the martyr, or the princess. In dreams, having the Black Madonna appear (as an archetype) connotes that you have within you an energy that carries the power to transform and heal whatever type situation you are experiencing. Whereas, having the wicked stepmother appear (as an archetypal energy), implies a warning to be wary of that which is going on around you.

Black Madonna: an archetypal sub-set of the Divine Feminine; a goddess; "the transcendent Kali-Mother, the black womb of light out of which all the worlds are always arising and to which they dissolve; the unknowable mystery behind all matter and all events; the 'darkness' of Divine love."

Chakra/s: a.k.a. energy mind centers, Chalices; non-anatomical vortexes of energy, spinning wheels of fiery energetic fuel. Revolving and moving freely, these wheels are designed to be conduits for the Sacred Energy of The One to move through out our being to power and empower our world and to connect us to the Cosmic Substance of the Universe; seven (or twelve) vertically aligned energy mind centers going from the base of the spine to the crown of the head and corresponding with specific body areas.

Chalice/Holy Grail: a symbolic representation of our innate quest for Truth; the cup of everlasting energetic nourishment that comes from God; the balance of the masculine and feminine natures; our body as a container for the energetic information system/energy mind centers, known in the Eastern traditions as the Chakras; a sacred cup believed to contain the blood of Jesus Christ; the Essence of who we are; a story created as a covert way to keep alive the secret message of the Divine Feminine.

Dreams: metaphorical portraits or pictures that our Higher Self paints in order that we might come to learn more about our self; the symbolic language of the subconscious mind revealed through sleep; the way to delve into the collective unconscious mind, the mind that stores all the beliefs and wisdom common to all cultures and societies.

Feminine, Divine: an archetype representing the feminine qualities and characteristics of The Divine Deity, God.

God: the One Presence and One Power; Universal Energy expressing; Higher Self; Higher Power; Spirit; That which is ultimately in "control" of our lives.

Head and Heart: the head represents the intellect and the heart represents intuitive knowing.

Holy Grail – Chalice: a sacred cup; a vessel; a cup said to contain the blood of Jesus Christ; the Essence of who we are; a story created as a covert way to keep alive the secret message of the Divine Feminine.

Ignorance: Ignorance is a state of a lack of understanding and of being unaware.

Love: the unconditioned Energy of Oneness; the universal glue that binds together humankind and all things.

Luminous Darkness: the space where the creative substance of the universe hovers, awaiting the call to do Its "work."; the "Silence."; the "*inner shrine*"; the place, from which ideas originate; involving the realm of Superconscious Mind; the playground of archetypes, dreams, and symbols; involving the realm of the subconscious mind/unconscious mind/personal and collective unconscious mind.

Masculine, Divine: an archetype representing the masculine qualities and characteristics of the Divine Deity, God.

Paradox: opposites; contradictions; complements, as in two sides of one coin.

***Shadow*:** stuck thought-forms and/or energetic blocks that reside within the subconscious mind and/or energy mind centers.

Sophia: feminine aspect of God; *Wisdom*; also, referred to in the Hebrew Testament by other names such as El Shaddai.

Subconscious/Unconscious Mind: : a memory bank; a storehouse of events for both the individual and for humankind; a.k.a., race consciousness or collective consciousness; a sensitive plate that sits behind the Super-Conscious and conscious minds, waiting to be imprinted by the thoughts we choose.

Theology: the study of God and/or religion that tends to honor a masculine-oriented sacred Being.

Thealogy: the study of God and/or religion that tends to honor a feminine-oriented sacred Being. (a coined word)

Void of Forgetfulness: a state of consciousness in which we forget and/or feel that we are not complete. We forget that synchronous resonance with the One is our true nature.

INDEX

A

B

C

D

E

F

G

H

I

J

K

L

BIBLIOGRAPHY

Baigent, Michael, Richard Leigh, and Henry Lincoln. *Holy Blood, Holy Grail.* New York: New York: Dell Publishing, 1983.

Begg, Ean C. M. *The Cult of the Black Virgin.* Boston, Massachusetts: Arkana, 1985.

Boehm, Toni G. *Embracing the Feminine Nature of the Divine: Integrative Spirituality Heralds the Next Phase of Conscious Evolution.* Greenwood, Missouri: Inner Visioning Press, 2002.*The Spiritual Intrapreneur.* Greenwood, Missouri: Inner Visioning Press, 2003.

Brown, Dan. *The Da Vinci Code: A Novel.* New York, New York: Doubleday, 2003.

Charpentier, Louis. *The Mysteries of Chartres Cathedral.* London, England: Thorston Publishers, 1972.

Eisler, Riane Tennenhaus. *The Chalice and the Blade: Our History, Our Future.* San Francisco, California: HarperCollins, 1987.

Engelsman, Joan Chamberlain. *The Feminine Dimension of the Divine.* Philadelphia, Pennsylvania: Westminster Press, 1979.

Filliette, Edith. *Saint Mary Magdalene, Her Life and Times.* Newton Lower Falls, Massachusetts: Society of Mary Magdalene, 1983.

Ford–Grabowsky, Mary. *Sacred Voices: Essential Women's Voices through the Ages.* San Francisco, California: HarperSanFrancisco, 2002.

Gustafson, Fred. *The Black Madonna,* Boston, Massachusetts: Sigo Press, 1990. *The Moonlit Path: Reflections on the Dark Feminine.* Berwick, Maine: Nicolas-Hays, 2003.

Harding, Mary Esther. *Women's Mysteries Ancient and Modern.* San Francisco, California: HarperCollins, 1976.

Harvey, Andrew. *Son of Man: The Mystical Path to Christ.* New York, New York: J. P. Tarcher/Putnam, 1999.

Mato, Tataya. *The Black Madonna Within: Drawings, Dreams, Reflections (Dreamcatcher).* Chicago, Illinois: Open Court Publishing, 1994.

Michell, John. *City of Revelation.* London, England: Garnstone Press, 1972.

Pagels, Elaine H. *The Gnostic Gospels.* New York, New York: Random House, 1979.

Qualls–Corbett, Nancy. *The Sacred Prostitute: Eternal Aspect of the Feminine.* Toronto, Canada: Inner City Books, 1988.

Starbird, Margaret. *The Goddess in the Gospels: Reclaiming the Sacred Feminine.* Santa Fe, New Mexico: Bear and Co., 1998.

———. *The Woman with the Alabaster Jar: Mary Magdalen and the Holy Grail.* Santa Fe, New Mexico: Bear and Co., 1993.

Stone, Merlin. *When God Was a Woman.* New York, New York: Dial Press, 1976.

Wallace-Murphy, Tim and Marilyn Hopkins. *Rosslyn: Guardian of the Secrets of the Holy Grail.* Boston: Element, 1999.

ABOUT THE AUTHOR

Toni G. Boehm, Ph.D., is an author, nurse, minister, and teacher on spirituality and mysticism. For fifteen years she served as the dean of administration for Unity School of Religious Studies at the world headquarters of Unity School of Christianity, Unity Village, Missouri; currently she is Director of Unity Institute and its Ministerial Education Program.

Teaching internationally, she facilitates classes and seminars on prayer, prosperity, personal growth, awakening the divine feminine in the 21st Century, and spiritual transformation. Boehm introduces students to the spiritual knowledge and skills necessary for living their lives from their highest innate potential. Her life work is devoted to "being a midwife for the birthing of the soul's remembrance." Through this work she assists others in personal awakenings in areas of:

* **transformation of consciousness** * **creativity and insight**
* **life's purpose and mission** * **prosperity**
* **prayer and prayer power** * **healing, forgiveness, and love**
* **self-empowerment** * **energy movement**

Boehm is a registered nurse; has a Bachelor of Arts in Health Care Education, from Ottawa University-Kansas; a Masters of Science in Nursing, from the University of Missouri; and a Ph. D. from Emerson Institute, CA. Boehm graduated from the University of Kansas Family Nurse Practitioner program, and the Unity School for Religious Studies, she is an ordained Unity minister.

Prior to joining the staff as dean at Unity School for Religious Studies, Boehm worked at the world headquarters of both the American Nurses Association and Hallmark Cards, Inc.

Boehm is past recipient of the University of Missouri, Kansas City Women's Council Award for Research. She is listed in Marquis' *Who's Who in American Women, Who's Who in America.* She has contributing chapters in:

• ***Sacred Voices: Essential Women's Wisdom through the Ages.*** **Mary Ford-Grabowsky. New York, New York: Harper Collins, 2002.**

• ***The Moonlit Path: Reflections on the Dark Feminine.*** **Fred Gustafson, editor. Berwick, Maine: Nicholas-Hays, 2003.**

Rev. Boehm is author of numerous articles and the books: ***The Spiritual Intrapreneur*** **(1996);** ***One Day My Mouth Just Opened—Reverie, Reflections and Rapturous Musings on the Cycles of a Woman's Life*** **(2000);** and ***Embracing the Feminine Nature of the Divine: Integrative Spirituality Heralds the Next Phase of Conscious Evolution*** **(2002)**.

For more information on her books go to **www.Amazon.com** or **www.BarnesandNoble.com**

For more information on tapes, CD's by the author, or to contact her go to **www.toniboehm.com**, (fax) 816-537-5254, or 816-304-3044 (cell)

FOOTNOTES

1 Toni G. Boehm, *Embracing the Feminine Nature of the Divine: Integrative Spirituality Heralds the Next Phase of Conscious Evolution* (Greenwood, Missouri: Inner Visioning Press, 2001), 89.

2 Ibid.

3 Fred Gustafson; editor; *The Moonlit Path,* Berwick, Maine: Nicholas-Hays, 2003, pg 22.

4 Andrew Harvey, *Son of Man: the Mystical Path to Christ,* Tarcher-Putnam, NY, pgs 192-193.

5 Fred Gustafason, *The Moonlit Path,* Nicholas-Hays, Berwick, ME., Chapter 12 by Toni G. Boehm, pg. 210.

6 Toni G. Boehm, *Embracing the Feminine Nature of the Divine;* Greenwood, MO., pgs., 207–214.

7 John J. Falone: *The Genius Frequency*, Global Light Network, Virginia Beach, VA., pgs 106-113.

8 Toni G. Boehm, *Embracing the Feminine Nature of the Divine*, Inner Visioning Press, Greenwood, MO.

9 Hillary Hart, *The Unknown She: Eight Faces of an Emerging Consciousness* (Inverness, California: The Golden Sufi Center, 2003), 202.

10 Ibid., 203.

11 Falone, John J.; *The Genius Frequency;* Global Light Network; Virginia Beach, VA.

12 Tim Wallace-Murphy and Marilyn Hopkins, *Rosslyn: Guardian of the Secrets of the Holy Grail* (Boston: Element Books, 1999), 193.

13 Carolyn Myss, *Anatomy of the Spirit: The Seven Stages of Power and Healing* (New York: Random House, 1997).

14 Wallace-Murphy, *Rosslyn,* 191.

15 Toni G. Boehm, *One Day My Mouth Just Opened,* Inner Visioning Press, Greenwood, MO.

16 Mary Ford-Grabowsky, *Sacred Voices: Essential Women's Voices through the Ages* (San Francisco, California: HarperSanFrancisco, 2002).

CPSIA information can be obtained at www.ICGtesting.com
Printed in the USA
LVOW062047220312

274298LV00002B/230/A

9 780970 153739